Running Silently

Running Silently

Betsy Waterman

with

Gary Waterman

Published by:
Simply Pets Books
620 South Orcas Street #80651
Seattle, Washington 98108

books@simplypetslifestyle.com
https://www.simplypetslifestyle.com

Cover Artist: Lauren N. Feil

ISBN: 978-1-7341932-2-0

The events and the people in this book are real,
but some names have been changed to protect individuals' privacy.

Table of Contents

Acknowledgments

This book was a labor of love. My late husband, Gary Waterman, started the story, but his death occurred before he could finish. I must start by thanking him, even though he will never read these words. If he had not had the idea of telling the story of our marvelous dogs and how we stumbled into the sport of skijoring, this book would have never existed. I would have moved forward after his death without having been able to read his funny and heartwarming stories of our lives and the misadventures of managing six lively dogs. Before he died, when he realized he would never have the chance to finish it himself, he asked me to finish his book. I thank him for his trust in me. I also was surprised and relieved to find a collection of notes he had made over the months he was confined to the hospital or homebound. They were filled with his memories of specific events and dates and made the finishing of this book after so many years possible. Thank you, Gary.

Many years passed following Gary's death when I would think about the book but found other things to distract me. It was my grown children, Lyndi Mott, Susan Kellar, Shelley Feil, Amy Albrecht, and Jeremy Waterman who would ask, from time to time, "How is the book coming, Mom?" They helped me to see that the finishing of this book was not only for Gary, but for all of the generations that followed him. Thank you all for your encouragement and shared joy as I completed it. I want to give a special thank you to Jeremy Waterman for his technical help in preparing the pictures in this book for publication. Just when he would think I had pulled out all the possible pictures I could ever want I would send him more and he graciously prepared them and sent them on to the editor for me. I also want to give a resounding thank you to my granddaughter, Lauren Nicole Feil who, despite struggling with a chronic and discouraging illness, agreed to do the drawing for the cover of this book. It meant the world to me, and I know it would have thrilled her grandfather.

Others helped in small ways and I want to acknowledge them here, as well. I want to thank David Sargent for gathering up all of the photographs that were still stored in his house and bringing them to my cabin. He also sent along some photos he had stored on his computer, especially the ones of Gracie as I could find none among my photos. I want to thank my friend, Gary Cranfield, who never met my late husband, but who understood the importance of this book to me and my family. He helped me dig out pictures, helped me with some technical issues, and patiently waited as I would write and rewrite, sometimes disappearing for hours. I also want to thank those who willingly let me use their actual names as first, Gary, and then I told the stories found in this book. Thank you to Andy Pierce, Max Chapman, David Sargent, Becky Oliver (who also did some early edits), Heather Emanuel, Roy Smith, Pat and Jay Chapman, Lauren Feil, Shelley Feil, Jeremy Waterman, Amy Albrecht, Christopher Feil, and Donald Balch. And although I did not use their names in the book, Gary's brother Phillip Waterman and his wife Marcia Waterman were critical to this story as it was Phillip who twice donated his bone marrow for Gary, and both were always there to support us in whatever way they could.

I want to thank Lisa Smith-Putnam from *Simply Pets Books* for taking a chance on publishing this book and who offered support and encouragement as we moved through the early publication process. If it weren't for a little video of an owl riding on an ice floe that went viral after I published it online, I would have never met her. She called me about doing a write-up about the owl for her magazine, *Simply Pets*. We talked and almost immediately connected as our discussion moved from the floating owl to our pets, and their importance in our lives. I took a deep breath and told her about Gary and my book, wondering if she might help give me some guidance on finding a publisher. I will be forever thankful to her for taking the time to take a look at the book and agreeing to publish it.

I also want to thank Janice F. McClintock who helped in the editing process and offered several helpful suggestions as well as designing the interior of the book. Thanks to Aundrea Hernandez for taking my granddaughter's lovely artwork and building a complete cover around it. Finally, I want to give a huge thank you to my editor, Lillie Ammann, who has helped me at every step of the publication process. Her careful editing, her specific and patient answers to my many questions, and most of all, her enthusiasm and belief in this book gave me the courage and confidence to take this book, that was my late husband's dream, and make it a story I dared to share.

Preface

This book has been a long time in the making. Eighteen years to be exact. Gary, whose voice you will hear through the first several chapters, died before the book, which he took such pride in, could be completed. I set out to finish this book, as I promised him, but it has taken much longer, and more courage, than I ever imagined.

When my husband Gary was first diagnosed with Acute Myelogenous Leukemia, he knew he was going to be spending long periods of time in the hospital, as the treatment completely wiped out the white blood cells. If he went home, he was at greater risk of contracting an infection that would further complicate his health. One day Gary, who to my knowledge had never written anything beyond the occasional college term paper, announced, "I think I will write a book about how a family who was steadfastly a one-dog family came to own six dogs."

"Wow!" I said. "That sounds like a great idea." But I didn't really expect him to do it. His typing skills were pretty slow, the project seemed pretty big, and he was fighting a devastating disease. I visited him often, but was still managing six dogs at home, had a small private practice as a licensed psychologist, and was a full-time professor at a nearby college. Often, I would arrive at his hospital room to find him taking notes or typing on his laptop. I didn't ask many questions about his progress on the book, and he didn't seem to want to share his work with me. I was co-editing a professional book of my own and contributing a couple of chapters to it, so sometimes we worked side by side, quietly immersed in what we were doing.

It was not until after he died that I realized how much, and how well, he had written about our life and our dogs. But he never had a chance to finish. After a year-long struggle, and after nearing the halfway mark of this book, he quietly died with family and friends by his side.

I moved on with my life. I missed him but determined to live a full and joy-filled life as he most certainly would have wished for me. My life was full of work, friends, and, of course, the care and training of our six dogs. The book always stayed just out of my vision, almost too painful for me to consider. I took a glance at it from time to time, surprised to learn he had actually enjoyed the hoopla I had always insisted on at Christmas and at which he mockingly rolled his eyes. Surprised at all he remembered and cherished of our life together. But, most of all, his book was about the dogs in our life and his profound and deep love for them. Nearly seventeen years after his death, I began reading his funny and poignant words and I knew I needed to finish his story.

PART 1:

GARY

Chapter 1

Ski Heaven

"5- 4 – 3 – 2 – 1! Go driver!" yelled the timekeeper.

"Hike! Hike! C'mon, Bayley! C'mon, Norm!" I shouted. With a jerk and a jump, we were off—me on skis with two dogs dragging a hapless human in their wake. I thought, *Oh please, please let me get around the first corner and out of sight before I fall.*

Fortunately, it was only about 200 meters to the first turn. My odds were good.

"Haw, Bayley! Haw, Norm!" We turned left and out of view.

"We made it. If I fall now, only one or two racers at most will see me," I said to myself. I was very relieved. As I settled in behind the dogs, I looked at the beauty around me. It was snowing, and I was part of the landscape.

Boy! I would never have thought I'd be here doing this. Only a few years ago, I didn't even know such a sport existed. *Where am I, and what am I doing?* That's the tale I'd like to share with you.

It's a true story. There may be a few details here and there that may not be exactly accurate, but I'm afraid that's due to a less-than-perfect memory, not fabrication. This tale revolves around my wife, me, and a little-known sport called skijoring.

Mostly, though, this story is about dogs—especially Bayley, our Border Collie, who was dubbed by one of his babysitters "the world's best dog." I'm sure there are many other dog owners out there who would dispute that designation, but read on and you will have to at least put him near the top of the list. Most of the other dogs in this story existed in our lives in one way or another because of what happened to Bayley.

But before we get to him, let's go back a bit. My wife, Betsy, and I live in Sandy Creek, New York, a small town about forty-five miles north of Syracuse. This puts us in the general area between Lake Ontario and the unique plateau called Tug Hill. Technically, Sandy Creek is not part of Tug Hill, but we're close enough. It's a wonderful place to live if you like to mountain bike, hike, canoe, cross-country ski, explore gorges, stream-walk, and, of course, skijor—all of which we enjoy immensely.

There are several factors making Tug Hill what it is. The major one is Lake Ontario. It is the smallest and deepest of the Great Lakes. Because it is so deep, it does not freeze over in the winter. Another related factor is the lay of the land. There is a steady rise in elevation from the eastern end of Lake Ontario, at 250 feet above sea level, to Gomer Hill, at 2,100 feet. Together they enable one of nature's greatest snow machines, a phenomenon called "Lake Effect."

"How good a machine?" you may ask. Well, it's not very often we make the national news, but in January of 1997, the Tug Hill town of Montague set a national record for the most snow in a twenty-four-hour period. The town received 77 inches. That's six and a half feet or two meters. Any way you measure it, it's a lot of snow. And that wasn't the end. Before the storm was over, the total amounted to 96 inches, equal to eight feet or just over two and a half meters. I'm sure this makes many of you cringe, but for those of us who enjoy winter sports, it gets our juices flowing. In fact, Tug Hill annually receives the most snow in the northeastern U.S., averaging over 200 inches, with some areas tallying even more.

Snow: Some people hate it; most people tolerate it. Then there are those of us who can't wait to see it come. I wasn't always like this. Until my mid-thirties, I was pretty much a couch potato. Then some friends invited Betsy and me to go cross-country skiing with them. They owned sixty-five acres and had made a few small trails. They had equipment we could borrow for the day. To be honest, I was less than enthusiastic about the whole thing. Still, they were serving chili and lots of other good food afterward, so why not?

Then something totally unexpected happened. I loved the sport. I didn't know it then, but this surprise infatuation would have a major impact on our lives.

❄ ❄ ❄

Something mystical happens when I put on my skis. I want to go as far as I can, as fast as I can. Of course, at first, that wasn't very far or very fast. But part of my soul had been taken over by this sport. Betsy, who skis technically much better than I do, had little trouble keeping up with me at first. Her attitude, however, is slightly different than mine when she skis. It's more like "Isn't it pretty out here in the crisp air Mother Nature provided?" I can't argue with that.

The Tug Hill region is one of the most strikingly beautiful places in the Northeast. Numerous hiking and biking trails run through the extensive state forests. Among the many streams, there are seventeen gorges (or "gulfs," as they are called around here). Some of them have walls that extend

300 feet above their stream beds. Strangely, even many locals don't know about them. We lived here almost thirty years before friends showed us some of them. These gulfs have not been exploited, which is just fine with the folks who enjoy their isolated beauty.

And, of course, there are the Lake Effect snowstorms. They can come and go quickly and are often only a few miles wide. These bands typically swing north and south, setting up in one place, then moving to another. Then they may move back to where they started. Sometimes a band will set up in one place and just stay there for a while; then, just as quickly as it started, it will stop. We have gone to bed at night under crystal clear skies and woken up under crystal clear skies, with two feet of fresh snow having accumulated in between. It's really amazing, and also quite beautiful. The sun comes up and shines through the barren trees with the surface of the snow sparkling like a bed of diamonds. Striking. Magical. In a few hours, the whole landscape has changed dramatically.

After that first Sunday afternoon on skis, Betsy and I knew we had to have some skis of our own. We debated whether to buy waxable or waxless skis, wooden skis or plastic. Betsy opted for wood (she's a kind of back-to-basics type) and developed a personal relationship with them almost at once, naming them "Kirsten" and "Karsten" for their Norwegian roots. I opted for a composite type, which is a fancy name for plastic. I named my skis "right" and "left." Both sets of skis were waxable. We made this choice when we were told waxable skis were faster. We were *both* drawn to faster.

The weather cooperated that first year. We had received a considerable amount of snow in January and February, but March was just cold. There was a well-maintained snowmobile trail that crossed the back edge of our property. I'd get home from work about 4:15 p.m., we'd put our skis on, and off we'd go. The great thing about this trail is, as soon as we turned back into the woods, the trail started downward. Not very much, but just enough to make it really fun. There was only one bad spot. Just as you left the woods and entered a meadow, there was a steep downhill stretch with a 90-degree turn in the middle. I have yet to negotiate that turn successfully. Betsy typically does it with ease. At least three or four times a week that March, we were able to squeeze in a twenty-to-thirty-minute ski at night. It was great.

I decided that to really enjoy the sport, I needed to exercise. I began working out during my lunch hours at work. All that next spring, summer, and fall I worked out religiously. I ran stairs. I rigged up a system of weights and pulleys in our basement to build my upper-body strength. I put on heavy boots and ankle weights and did kicking exercises, which I thought mimicked the motions of a classical skier. I was turning into Macho Skier!

Betsy, on the other hand, had neither the time nor the desire to devote to the same type of regimen. In 1982, she decided to go back to school and complete her undergraduate degree, which she did the following year. In 1986, she completed her Master's plus CAS in School Psychology, and in 1990, she received her Ph.D. in School Psychology. While her exercise regimen may have been haphazard at best, she did maintain a good level of overall health, and she was still able to ski right along.

The first few winters, we frequently skied with friends. There were a few winters where, for one reason or another, we just couldn't get out much. The gap between our relative strength was not obvious. By 1986, though, most of our friends were not skiing much, if at all. Betsy was just starting a very tough Ph.D. program. I was becoming less satisfied with my job. The winter of '86 was not very satisfying. Betsy still wanted to ski. I still wanted to ski. Our ideas of going skiing, however, were very different.

Betsy loved a good three-to-five-kilometer ski. Unfortunately, at that distance, I felt like I was just warming up. We alternated our martyrdom. I would sigh and turn back toward the car, stopping at a far shorter distance than I wanted because it was what Betsy wanted. Or Betsy would push on—muttering quietly under her breath about how skiing was supposed to be fun, not work—because it was what I wanted. (She maintains that she never whines. Just for the record, she clearly does). I'm sure some of you are wondering why we just didn't go off separately. But we don't operate this way. We do things together. We enjoy doing things together. We're each other's best friends. Still, this was becoming a major stressor.

Enter Leo. Leo was our Belgian Sheepdog. Leo was born February 21, 1986. We named him after King Leopold of Belgium, a nineteenth-century despot. We didn't know he was a despot when we named Leo. We had just run across the fact that there had been a King Leopold of Belgium. King Leopold of Belgium was a bad, bad man. King Leopold of Waterwood (that's the name of our home property) was a great, great dog.

Belgians are beautiful dogs, all black with a square body. They typically weigh from fifty-five to seventy pounds. Intelligent, strong, and brave, they are frequently used in Europe as police dogs and guard dogs. During World War I, they were trained as messengers. In this country, they are primarily pets. You would think they would make great watch dogs. Not Leo. Though somewhat intimidating in appearance, Leo gleefully greeted everyone who came to our house and enthusiastically invited them in.

Leo

Leo was bright, lively, and more than a little mischievous. He had us very well trained. He quickly trained us to give him a treat if we wanted him to come into the house. We cleverly taught him to come running toward the house when we called, and then dance merrily just out of reach until we had reentered the house and retrieved some unhealthy doggy tidbit with which to entice him. The calls: "Leo, Leo. Come 'ere boy. Leo, would you like some cheese? I have cheese for you, boy." (To Leo, cheese was a generic term for treat, though in fact, cheese did work best.) Leo would appear after a while. Then, making sure we did indeed have a treat for him, he would come to us. In our defense—and to support the notion that we were nearly as bright as our pet—we could sometimes trick him into entering by leaving open the door to the house. He'd come streaking in when he heard the door to the refrigerator open. We felt some perverse sense of pride in having outsmarted our dog. Looking back on it now, I can only think, *How pathetic.*

Leo liked to play other games. One of his favorites was a variation of hide and seek: He hid things, and we had to find them. One of the problems with this game was that Leo never told us when he was playing. His favorite things to hide were leather work gloves and hammers.

You see, we were constantly upgrading our house. Betsy loved to tear out walls—who doesn't? At some point, I ceased to be surprised when I came home from work and found a wall missing. I did point out which walls were load-bearing walls, so at least our house wouldn't fall down. Remodeling is one thing—rebuilding quite another. Anyway, Leo made any remodeling project more challenging. Leo seemed to know that the hammer was a key tool. I would start a job, and when I laid down my hammer, Leo would appear, acting mildly curious. The next thing I'd know, both Leo and the hammer were missing. Of course, he did this with a great deal of skill. The first few times this happened, I didn't think much of it. After all, it's not unusual for me to go get something, take the hammer along, and lay it down somewhere. Usually when that happened, I could retrace my steps and find it fairly quickly. Naturally, I would go through the standard questions:

"Where'd I lay that darned thing?"

"Betsy, have you seen my hammer?" (The real message here being, "you've taken my hammer; where did you put it?") It's always good to have someone to blame. Besides, my wife is somewhat fanatical about picking things up. On more than one occasion she put my morning juice glass in the dishwasher before I even had time to pour myself any orange juice. So you can understand why she was a suspect here.

"No, hon, but I'll help you look for it. Where have you looked?"

"All the normal places." (This happened even before Leo.)

"Did you look outside?" Betsy continued.

"I haven't been outside."

"If you've looked everywhere inside, we might as well look outside."

I was doing this particular project in the summer. I suppose I could have wandered outside for some reason and just not remembered.

"You're right," I said.

Sure enough, there was the hammer, laying against the outside entrance to the basement. I didn't remember being there at all; I was quite perplexed. This project went on and off for a couple of weeks. Several more times my hammer turned up missing. Each time I found my hammer in the same place. Betsy and I became suspicious. It was either some supernatural occurrence … or Leo. Could it be that man's best friend was a practical joker?

We knew Leo liked to bury things. Betsy once observed him take three pieces of dog food, carefully bury them, and then proceed to various parts of the yard to make sure they were sufficiently camouflaged from all angles. We added up all the circumstantial evidence. Leo had long since learned to open the screen doors, so the fact that the hammer was outside in summer was not surprising. The hammer was always in the same place. Leo liked to play games. We decided to put Leo outdoors when I was working and—what do you know—the missing hammer problem disappeared.

Leo, however, was not easily discouraged. He needed a new challenge, and I provided him with it: leather gloves. When I worked outside or was tearing out old lumber from the house, I wore gloves. You'd think after the hammer incidents that we would learn. Nope. When my gloves started to go missing, we were mystified. The amazing thing is that Leo stole only the right-hand gloves. At one point, I had a large collection of left-hand gloves. What made this harder to prove is that Leo got smarter. He buried the evidence. It was only when my wife caught him in the act that we were able to figure out where all the gloves had gone. Other than the one glove Betsy spotted him burying, we were never able to find any of the other stolen gloves. He was, after all, very careful when he buried something.

Leo loved life. But more than anything else in the whole, wide world, Leo loved to skijor. *Skijor*, very roughly translated from Norwegian, means "an animal that pulls a person on skis." Today dogs provide the horsepower, but in the past, reindeer and horses were used for this purpose. Of course, we didn't know any of that when Leo and Betsy began their love affair with skijoring. In fact, neither Betsy nor I even knew such a sport existed. We, like most people in the world, had never heard of such a thing.

We discovered Leo's love for skijoring quite by accident. Betsy decided to take Leo along with us on one of our ski outings. Our plan was for Leo to be on his leash and run along beside Betsy. We both got our skis on and prepared to go. When Betsy said "Okay, Leo, let's go," she was not even close to ready for what happened next. Leo exploded forward, and within a few seconds, they both disappeared over the horizon. I took chase. Kick, pole, kick, pole.

Over the first little hill, about 200 meters from the start, a trail called Winona Way turns right off the unplowed Wart Road. Our plan was to take this trail. But as I broke over the hill, I didn't see them. I got to Winona Way and looked up the trail. There they were, coming back to get me. As we approached each other, I could see Leo's face. I've never seen such sheer joy in a face in all my life. Betsy, too, had a smile as wide as Leo's. I knew that, as long as Leo was around, I wouldn't have to worry about Betsy lagging behind. Suddenly, I seemed incredibly slow.

By the time Betsy and Leo got back to me, Leo's initial burst was done, and I was able to hang a little closer to them. This arrangement worked well for the next nine years: Betsy giving the command to go, Leo leaping into his harness, and me watching their backsides quickly disappear over the first small hill. After a while, I would see them coming back to get me, with an expression on their faces that said: "You are really slow, but because we're nice, we'll slow down and ski with you now."

Only once did we have a problem. Betsy and Leo met up with another skier and his dog that was running loose. Without warning or provocation, this dog, about the same size as Leo, grabbed Leo by the throat and then began ripping his ear. Betsy, skis and all, threw herself between them. In the fray, she was bitten above her left eye. Leo and Betsy were both bleeding into the snow, with the other dog's owner standing helplessly by. And the dog continued its attack. I tried getting them apart with my poles, but to no avail. The other dog's owner continued to be ineffective.

I finally managed to get my skis off, and a well-placed kick to the attacking dog's groin was enough of a distraction to allow us to pull them apart. Please understand I do not advocate kicking dogs as a way of controlling behavior, but two individuals I loved were being hurt. The dog's owner, looking at my wife's rapidly swelling eye and Leo's dangling ear, mumbled apologies.

"I'm really sorry," he said. "He's normally good around other dogs. He's very friendly. I don't know what got into him. I'm really sorry. Are you okay?"

"I'll be all right," Betsy responded.

Actually, she wasn't. Though it didn't appear to be much of a wound at first, by the time we made it back to the parking lot, the swelling was so bad she could not see out of that eye at all. Naturally, she refused to go to the emergency room. We iced it, and I did convince her to go to the doctor's office the next day. Leo's ear was repaired by the vet. But some scars remained in both my wife's and Leo's hearts. To this day, Betsy still struggles with a moment of panic when she sees a loose dog on the trail.

Although in this case Leo was clearly not the aggressor, there were times when, under harness, he could be unpleasant to other dogs when he was pulling, though he was always friendly to people. We don't know why. Perhaps he felt more vulnerable under harness and thus more threatened. Maybe he was just so focused, he didn't want to be disturbed. We never will know.

After this incident, Betsy became extremely vigilant. As soon as she saw another dog approaching, she reeled in Leo's line and held him tight. This worked well, except when a dog decided to trail along. Usually, though, Leo settled down after a few minutes, and we continued with our ski.

Since we still didn't know that Leo's towing of Betsy on skis was actually a sport with a name, we had tossed around our own ideas about how to set up Leo so the pulling would not put any stress on his neck. We also were looking for how Betsy could use her poles to help Leo along, which meant finding a way to free her hands from holding the leash. At first, we got him a lightweight harness you can buy at any department store. After one use, we realized this setup was not good. The narrow straps dug into Leo's neck, and Betsy still had to use a regular leash. We decided to go to our local Agway store. They could order us a heavy-duty harness with lambswool lining the front and top and D-rings on the side to attach traces, lines that run from the harness back to the driver. It seemed like a good setup to us.

Remember, we were still pretty ignorant about this whole thing. Turned out it was a good setup for pulling a cart, but not for skijoring. For one thing, both hands are tied up holding the traces, preventing the driver from using her poles. For another, it seemed to upset the rhythm of the dog to have two traces dangling down on his side. You could never keep the tension evenly distributed. Betsy knew she had to make some modifications.

By tying the traces together across Leo's back, Betsy jury-rigged the system so there was one line coming from above Leo's rear hips. She then connected the two traces at the end with a red leash and pulled the whole thing up around her waist. This worked fine as long as Leo was pulling steadily, but as Leo began to tire and his pace slowed, the traces and leash would slip to her ankles—which can be dangerous for a skier. She would try to cope by poling with one hand and holding the traces up with the other, looking pretty silly and rendering poling generally ineffective. There was also no quick way to escape the contraption, if, for example, she was skiing downhill on ice and rapidly overtaking the dog.

She talked about attaching Velcro to the traces and to her jacket but never quite got to that point. In fact, while she doesn't like to admit it, she skijored for nine years with this rather inconvenient setup. Remember, though, she didn't know she was engaging in a sport at the time. She just knew

Leo was pulling her on skies. The realization didn't come until one day she encountered a stranger on the trail who said, "Wow—you're skijoring." Betsy nodded yes and then went home to search out what the woman meant.

I finally purchased a book for Betsy called *Skijor with Your Dog* by Mari Hoe-Raitto, and we realized there was special equipment made for just what we were doing. Betsy's system had the right idea, but with a couple of glaring pitfalls.

Today, we use X-back harnesses on our dogs. These are lightweight and strong. Also, the harness comes to a point at the rear of the dog, providing even pulling. The biggest difference in my wife's system and a real system comes behind the dog. The line between the dog and the driver has two important features. First, there is a bungee section. This provides a smoother take-off as the dogs blast away from the start. It also smooths out the entire give-and-take between driver and dog. This is useful when you need to snowplow with your skis to slow or stop the dogs, or, as is often in my case, when I fall. (I fall a lot, and I've gotten quite good at it.) The other important feature is a quick release. This is again useful when I fall. Last, there is a padded belt for the driver instead of one that falls to your ankles if the dog begins to let up on pulling. Definitely an improvement.

Leo loved to pull. No, it was more than that. Leo *lived* to pull. If we left the front closet open, Leo would drag his harness out of the closet, drop it at our feet, and look at us as if to say, "Okay, I'm ready. Let's go. C'mon, the snow's a-waitin." It didn't matter if it was the middle of summer. To Leo, snow was always a possibility. Unfortunately, more often than not, we had to say, "Sorry, big fella, we can't go right now." Leo would then drop his head, go to one of his favorite spots, lie down, and let out a big sigh. At the same time, he would give us one of those looks that asked, "Are you sure we can't go today? I'm ready whenever you are …." We'd feel compelled to answer, "It's okay, Leo. We'll go again soon." Leo didn't find much consolation in this, but he accepted it with guilt-rendering resignation.

Leo lived to pull, but alas, dogs do not live as long as humans. During the winter of 1994–1995, when Leo was ten years old, he began to noticeably slow down. He also began to limp a little on his right front leg from time to time. Still, we managed to get in some good skis. By the next winter, though, we knew Leo's pulling days were over. We tried to take him a couple of times. Leo still got that twinkle in his eye, still danced about when we got out his harness, though somewhat stiff-legged. He still threw himself into his harness at start-up, but after only a few hundred yards, he was simply too tired to go on. We took him home and hung his harness for the last time. He laid down, exhausted. He seemed more than sad. He seemed defeated.

Leo spent one more spring and summer with us. We had added to our canine numbers by acquiring Bayley as a tiny puppy. He was the son of our daughter's Border Collie. This was a big deal for my wife, who loved dogs but, to this point, felt they should be enjoyed one at a time. Knowing that Leo was aging, though, and hearing on some animal show that it was good to socialize a puppy with a mature dog, we broke the one-dog-at-a-time barrier. Leo tolerated Bayley's puppy antics and spent most of his time as an interested but passive observer. In September of 1996, Leo's limp suddenly got worse. We decided to take him to the vet. We were hoping to get him some pain medication for what we thought was arthritis. I took him.

"How long has he been like this?" asked Dr. O.

"He'd limp from time to time, but it's suddenly gotten a lot worse," I responded.

"Has he twisted it or banged it somehow?"

"No, I don't think so. We think it's just arthritis."

"Hmmm. I think we'd better take a picture of it."

Dr. O. left, and a veterinary technician came in to get Leo.

"C'mon boy," she said. "Let's go get your picture taken." She led him away. "Boy, he really is limping pretty badly."

I looked at him. "Man!" I thought. "It seems worse than ever."

Leo looked back at me.

"I'll be right here, boy," I said, trying to comfort him.

I waited in the exam room. I sat. I stood. I looked at a poster on the wall that listed 100+ breeds of dogs by country and origin. It had a picture and thumbnail sketch of each one. I sat again. The vet tech led Leo in, followed by Dr. O. The tech gave me Leo and left.

"Hi, boy. Hi, Leo. How're you feelin', fella?" Even though it had been only a few minutes, we were still happy to see each other.

Dr. O. clipped the X-ray up on the white, lighted piece of glass made for just such a purpose and circled the right front shoulder joint with his pointer.

"See this area?" he asked.

I was a massage therapist, and I knew enough about anatomy and joints to know it didn't look good.

"You see this large, white area here, and it kind of stars out?" he continued. "That's the classic pattern of bone cancer."

A chill ran up my back.

"Now, it's possible that it's an infection," the doctor said, unconvincingly.

"Do you really think it could be?" I asked.

He hedged. "Once in a while, an infection will look like this. I mean, you said he's been limping on and off for a couple of years, and bone cancer doesn't take that long."

I could tell he didn't believe it. Leo's sister from another litter had died of the same thing at about the same age. We both knew what had to be done.

"We could do it now if you want."

"No," I said. "I want to talk this over with Betsy. I know she will want to see him again."

That day was Wednesday, September 3, 1997—our thirty-first wedding anniversary. I couldn't take the thought of saying goodbye on our anniversary. I took him home. Betsy came out of her office from a therapy session with a client (she was a licensed psychologist with a small private practice) to ask about Leo.

"How did everything go?" she asked.

"Not good," I responded. "It's not arthritis. It's bone cancer."

Betsy's face fell. "Oh no," she said. "That's what Jennifer's dog died of. They diagnosed it and she had her put down within a few days."

"You're right," I said. "I had forgotten that it happened so quickly."

"I have to get back to my client. We'll talk more when I get a break."

Betsy went back to her client. I felt sorry for her. She was the one who needed counseling at that moment. After ten years of being a team, a special bond had developed between Leo and Betsy.

Betsy's break came later that day. There wasn't much discussion. We both knew. I think Leo knew, too. I called and made the appointment for Friday morning, a time when both of us could be there.

It's never easy to decide to euthanize a pet. Neither one of us slept that night. It was our anniversary, and all we could think about was Leo. Were we doing the right thing?

The answer came the next day. Leo could barely move. He managed to get up a few times to go outside, but that was all. Thursday night was horrible. Leo lay next to our bed, moaning in pain most of the night. Bayley, our now year-and-a-half-old Border Collie, recognized Leo's distress. Bayley stayed at Leo's side, and when Leo moaned, Bayley gently licked his face. Leo would look at him as if to say, "It's up to you now, Bayley. They're good humans. Take good care of them."

At the appointed time the next morning, we took Leo to the vet for the last time.

"This doesn't hurt him at all," said the vet. It wasn't Dr. O. He was out on call.

"We know," we both said.

"It's just an overdose of anesthesia. It really is like going to sleep" she said, trying to reassure us.

"We know," we both said. "Goodbye Leo. Goodbye ol' pal."

It was done. I cried. Betsy cried. The vet cried.

We went home.

Leo loved to pull.

Chapter 2

Hunting for a Hunter

Bayley was born May 11, 1996. It's an easy day to remember. It was the day before Mother's Day. It was a near-perfect spring day, sunny, with temperatures in the 60s. Betsy got an early-morning call from our daughter that Puzzles, Bayley's mother, had begun delivery. I was away at an all-day workshop, honing my skills as a massage therapist, and Betsy had to participate in graduation exercises at the college where she taught. She raced back to see how things were progressing.

It had all started several weeks earlier, when our daughter Amy had decided she wanted to breed Puzzles when the time was right. She did some research about breeding her dog, and felt the next time that Puzzles went into heat would be the perfect time. At the time, Amy was living with a cousin and a high school friend in a rented house in Pulaski, about seven miles from our home near Sandy Creek. We had heard about a possible stud for Puzzles from someone my wife knows. Through her practice as a psychologist, in addition to helping a great number of people, Betsy gets a great deal of useful information. Betsy made the call. A woman answered—Mrs. M.

"I understand that you may have a male Border Collie that you might let us use as a stud," Betsy said.

"Yup," said the woman. "I did have a pair, but the female died a year ago last fall." [That's autumn of 1994, for those of you who are keeping track.] "He's not done anything in a while. He's not much to look at these days. He's lost a lot of hair and is bald in some spots. When he was young, though, he was quite the looker. He's nearly eleven now."

"Oh," said Betsy, conjuring up some rather interesting images. Then she suddenly had a new worry.

"Would it be dangerous for him to act as a stud?" she asked. Betsy was beset with a picture of the dog, bent on breeding a young energetic Border Collie, falling over dead from a heart attack. This was immediately followed with another concern.

"Do you think the sperm would be normal?" Betsy was now envisioning strangely formed little puppies—or no puppies at all.

"I don't know," was the succinct answer.

"I think I will check with our vet," Betsy said.

She did. The vet reassured her that, if the dog was healthy and willing, there really should be no danger to either the aging stud dog or the potential puppies.

Betsy called the owner back. The hope was that the stud was a working dog or, at least, had been a working dog. So Betsy inquired, "Does he do any sheep herding?"

"No sheep. We used to have some cows. I'd say 'Go get the cows' and off he'd go. Pretty soon, he and the girls [cows] would be headed to the barn. Never had no training, neither. The only problem is sometimes he'd get bored and he'd just go get the cows and put 'em in the barn. I'd put 'em back out in the pasture, and the next thing you'd know, he'd have 'em back in the barn. Darndest thing."

That would be the untrained part. Anyone who has ever seen a Border Collie herd sheep or cows may wonder, *How do they get them to do that?* Betsy and I wondered that the first time we saw a demonstration. The fact is, the behaviors they exhibit—the stance, the drop, the way they circle, the eye contact, and the intense focus—are all what make a Border a Border. When you combine this with speed, intelligence, and impressive athletic ability, you have the ingredients for a near-perfect herding machine. The trainer's challenge is to get the Border to do all these things on command, and *only* on command.

A friend's Border Collie offered some great examples of these natural behaviors. Their dog, Star, herded everything. She doesn't play fetch. She plays "herd the ball"—or Frisbee, or stick, or whatever one may choose to throw or kick. Instead of chasing after the designated fetch object, she runs a large half-circle, ending up where the fetch has come to rest, takes the Border stance, stares at it and glances back at the thrower as if to say, "Here it is. I know it tried to get away from you, but I have it stopped now. You can come get it." And she would stay focused on the fetch until you either came to get it or released her.

But the most fun was to watch Star with cats. I know this may bother you cat people a bit, but rest assured, she has never hurt a cat. There was one time when a neighbor's cat crossed Star's path. The cat took off for his favorite tree. Star sprang into action. Instead of chasing the cat in the traditional way—that would be no challenge at all—Star did the Border Collie circle thing. The cat looking back, and not seeing Star behind him, thought he had it made.

"Stupid dog," he thought. "This isn't how you chase a cat. I'll be up that tree in no time flat. That'll show that dumb dog a thing or two."

Tsk, tsk, silly kitty. Star isn't chasing you; she's *herding* you. Just as the cat was preparing to leap into the tree, Star appeared face to face with the cat, who froze in his tracks. Star stared him down for a few moments, then pranced away. Point made. Never underestimate a Border Collie!

Betsy continued with the conversation. "Good," she said. "How much do you charge for a stud fee?"

"Well, let me see. Like I said, it's been a while." She paused for a moment. Then, in the background, Betsy could hear her discussing it with her husband. Then she turned back to the phone. "A hundred and fifty dollars, and you'll have to come fetch 'im and bring 'im back when he's done. If nothing happens, I won't charge you anything."

"Great. Thanks," Betsy responded. "We expect her to go into heat pretty soon."

"Yup," came the reply. "Give us a call when she's ready."

We didn't have to wait long. Puzzles went into heat shortly thereafter. We called and got directions to the owner's house. It was a cold winter day, even for mid-March. We arrived at the farm. It was located in a part of New York that is flat, open farmland, so there is nothing to slow the wind coming off Lake Ontario, some thirty miles to the west. We found their farm, approached the small, nondescript house, and knocked on the door.

A man greeted us. "Come on in," he said cheerfully. "Well, there he is."

"Whoa!" I thought as the dog emerged from under a desk near the door. Borders seemed to like to lie underneath things. He got up much the same way I get out of bed in the morning—a little stiff.

"He's got a bit of arthritis, so he doesn't pop up like he used to," said Mr. M.

Once up, though, he gave us that typical Border welcome—tail wagging, a great big welcoming smile on his face, and an expression that said, "Look, Mom and Dad, someone has come to visit. Isn't that wonderful?"

"His name's Charlie," said Mrs. M.

"Oh, what a good boy you are. Yes you are. You're such a good boy," Betsy and I said as we leaned over and greeted him.

He responded by becoming even more enthusiastic, wagging his whole body and sort of leaping about (the arthritis, remember).

He wasn't exactly as we had pictured him. In some ways, better; in some ways, well … different. He wasn't nearly as bald as we had pictured, but he was shorter-legged and broader-chested than we had imagined him. It was not our vision of what the classic Border Collie should look like—slim and long-legged, with a white collar, chest, and tummy. But we were still new at this Border Collie thing. We didn't quite realize at the time the number of variations possible. For the health of the breed, this is a good thing. It's when a group of people get together and decide upon some artificial standard of what a certain breed should look like that the overall quality of the breed may start to deteriorate. He was virtually all black except for his telltale white-tipped tail and little, white slippers on three feet.

"I don't know if my wife told you or not when you called, but his mate of ten years died a year ago last fall," said Mr. M.

"Yes, she had mentioned it."

"It was awful," he continued. "After she died, he just moped around here. He wouldn't do anything. Wouldn't eat. He lost weight. He just laid there. We were really worried about him. Then, last spring, I got the lawn mower out. My wife said as soon as he heard the mower start, his head popped up, his

25

ears perked up, and he almost ran to the door. Next thing I know, he's running round and round the mower. He always loved to do that. He's been fine ever since." Then he looked at us and said, somewhat philosophically, "Funny what brings them back, sometimes, isn't it?" referring to animals and people in general.

"I'm sure he'll do the job for you. He's a good dog." Then he turned to Charlie and said, "You be a good boy now. I'll see you in a few days."

He handed us the leash, and Charlie, a little hesitant at first, came along willingly. He popped up into the car like it was no big deal and was soon perched on the back seat, looking quite happy to be going on an adventure.

The ride home was uneventful. Charlie sat up for a while, looking around, enjoying the ride. Borders, in fact most dogs, love to ride. Once when we were visiting a local lumber yard, some people were exercising their dogs in a field across the way. Soon, they were putting their dogs back in their truck. In a flash, Bayley jumped out of our car, ran at great speed across a parking lot, through a field, and leaped into the back of the truck with the other dogs just as they were getting ready to raise the back gate of the truck. The people with the truck seemed a little stunned at first, having no idea from where this dog had dropped in. Betsy and I finally caught up with our dog, who looked out at us as if to say, "I'm just going for a bit of a ride. I'll be right back." Fortunately, after feeling a little embarrassed, we all had a good laugh. But, of course, in this story, with Charlie riding in the back seat, Bayley hasn't been born (or, as I think of it, even conceived yet).

The breeding process went fairly smoothly. We introduced Charlie to Puzzles, and after several hours of checking him out, Puzzles decided Charlie was okay. (This is not always the case.) Star, who was the same age as Puzzles, went into heat nine days after Puzzles. Star's owners figured since we had such good luck with Charlie that they would also use him. When Star went into heat, they also drove to pick up the aging stud Charlie. They brought him home and introduced him to Star. Nothing doing. Star didn't have one iota of interest in Charlie. She had her eye on the brown dog next door. Charlie would approach her and Star would simply turn away. Her owners were getting a little discouraged.

Then came the big break. They had taken the family, including the dogs, on an adventure. Star had been as disinterested in Charlie as ever, of course. When they got home, however, Star hopped out of the car and saw the brown dog. She couldn't help herself, and she raised her tail enticingly. Charlie, ever the opportunist, seized the moment. In a flash, Star and Charlie were together. Charlie may have been old, but when presented with the proper motivation, he could still muster up a little quickness.

A little more than two months after Charlie's visit, Puzzles delivered seven of the cutest puppies ever to bless this planet. There were four males and three females. At birth, all were mostly black with little white markings on each one's neck. The exception was Bayley. He was considerably whiter than the others and was marked much like his mother. None of them had the full white collar that Betsy and I were sort of hoping for. Still, this was a relatively small matter. All of them had the distinctive white-tipped tail typical of Border Collies. All were exceptionally cute.

I wish that I could say that Puzzles was a wonderful mother. The best you could say is that Puzzles was a *dutiful* mother. Take, for example, feeding time. With her, it was like "Mommy's here to feed you. Please attach yourselves and let's get this over with"—as opposed to "Okay, all you sweet little things, Mommy's here to feed you and spend some quality time with you." That just wasn't Puzzles. She fed them, kept them clean, and in her own neurotic way, I believe she did love them.

When they first started to leave the nest, it drove her crazy. She kept trying to bring them back. When the pups were only three or four weeks, this became an impossible task, and Puzzles let them wander into the relative security of the kitchen. I think when Puzzles realized they'd be safe there, she became a little more relaxed. And when the pups were weaned, she seemed to breathe a huge sigh of relief.

Then, of course, there was the problem of naming them. For each of our children, Betsy and I had spent months pondering what name to give each child. Now, all of a sudden, we needed seven names. Luckily, we only needed temporary names, since five of the seven were going to go to new homes. We still needed to come up with something other than "that one over there," or "you know, the next to the biggest one." We eventually started calling them by their distinctive markings. The larger males, twins, were called "One Spot" and "Two Spot." In fact, this slight difference in marking was the only way we could tell them apart. Amy decided to keep the smallest female and called her Crescent because of a nearly perfectly shaped crescent on the back of her neck. She was the only one to keep her temporary name. The largest female I called Stealth. Her marking looked like the profile of a stealth bomber. No one really liked the name, but no one came up with anything better, either. Bayley, I'm sad to say, we called Pig—and it wasn't because of the way he ate. In fact, Bayley was frequently the last to eat. Nope. He just looked like a little pig—a cute little pig, but a pig, nonetheless. The other two I simply don't remember.

Pig, a.k.a. Bayley, may have been the last to eat, but he was the first out of the nest. Perhaps because he couldn't get to a nipple, he decided he might as well explore his world. At any rate, when his eyes were barely opened, we found him in the middle of the kitchen floor, away from the safety of the kitchen closet. This was somewhat distressing for Puzzles, who really wanted to keep all of her children together but was held down by six suckling puppies. Amy rescued Bayley and put him back with the others, who by this time had had their fill, and now left room for Bayley to eat.

Puppyhood went smoothly. When they were weaned at about eight weeks, we moved them from the kitchen closet to the side porch. Puppies are cute, but they do leave an odor some might consider offensive. Also at this point, Puzzles figured she had done her part and pretty much gave up on the mothering thing. She was quite relieved to give up the responsibilities to us. I don't want you to get the wrong idea about Puzzles. It wasn't that she disliked her offspring. It was just the pressure of being a mother that was hard for her.

The most memorable event of their early puppyhood came when they were nearly six weeks old. We went to visit with Star's family. As you may recall, Star went into heat short-ly after Puzzles, and sure enough, nine days after Puzzles had her pups, Star had four pups. We decided to take all the dogs for a walk. If you do the math, you'll come up with eleven puppies and two adult dogs. In addition, there were two chil-dren, aged six and thirteen; their mom and dad; Amy; Betsy; and me to manage the mass of Border Collies. It seemed like we had died and gone to Border Collie heaven. It must have been quite a scene to the casual observer to see us coming along the street. The biggest challenge was keeping the leashes untangled. Dogs, especially puppies, don't always travel in a straight line. It was a walking Border Collie kaleidoscope. People came out of their houses to point and chuckle, and by the time we were returning home, we had a small group of children following us, much to the delight of the puppies and the concern of Puzzles and Star.

When the puppies reached eight weeks old, it was time for them to find their forever homes. Amy had decided to keep Crescent, but we were still undecided as to which pup we wanted to keep. It came down to choosing between Stealth and Pig. This was not an easy decision. Each had their own endearing qualities. Pig was curious and adventuresome. He also looked the most like his mother. Stealth was, well … she just had a quality about her that's hard to put your finger on. We decided to let fate handle the matter. If someone wanted Stealth, we would keep Pig. If someone wanted Pig, we would keep Stealth.

Fate played with us a little. As it turned out, the last two pups available were Stealth and Pig. A nice family came and chose Stealth. They wanted a female. I was surprised at my reaction. When the other four pups went to their new owners, I was happy for them. When Stealth left, I had a real feeling of loss. I felt like saying "Wait. We've changed our minds. We don't want to sell either of the dogs." But I didn't say anything. I shed a little tear and watched her leave. Later, Betsy told me that she felt the same way. We often wish that we had kept both Pig and Stealth, but we didn't, and that's that.

When you sell puppies, you wonder what happened to them. We have heard from three of the five owners. One Spot was renamed Comet and was reported to entertain his family in wonderful ways. Two Spot was renamed Nelix and turned into an incredible Frisbee dog. And Stealth? She was taken to be trained to herd sheep. Her trainer was very impressed with both her looks and her ability. In fact, he wanted to know who her parents were, because he was convinced that she was related to one of his best dogs. We still miss her, but it helps knowing she is doing what a Border Collie was born to do.

Pig would never do as a permanent name. Somehow, coming up with a name became a major challenge. Then, one day while we were visiting some friends, I saw a bottle of Bailey's Irish Crème. "Bailey." I thought, "That's a good name for a Border Collie, being that it is Irish and all. I'll run it by Betsy and see what she thinks." I didn't know at the time that Bailey was primarily a girl's name. On the other hand, in this day of unisex everything, what the hey? It's a name.

Betsy also liked the name. She decided to spell the name with a "y" instead of an "i." It seems there's some psychological test written by someone named Bayley. That's okay with me. It adds a little character. So why not?

Bayley's early puppyhood was mostly uneventful. Bayley tried to get Leo to play with him, but Leo was getting old and didn't feel the need or obligation to play with Bayley. Bayley's favorite game was grabbing Leo's tail. Bayley would pull until Leo got up and pulled him around. When Leo got tired of this, he would put a move on Bayley that would cause Bayley to let go. We never quite saw exactly what he did. Then Leo would quickly lay down in such a way as to make his tail unavailable. Though he never admitted it, I think Leo enjoyed the game as much as Bayley did.

Amy frequently brought Puzzles and Crescent to our place to play with Bayley. With forty acres, there was plenty of room for them to run, and Borders love to run. Unfortunately, Bayley was not as fast as either Puzzles or Crescent. Thus, after a few minutes of the three of them running, we would hear "Yip! Yip! ... Yip! Yip!" from Bayley pleading "Mom ... Sis ... Wait! I can't keep up with you. Slow down! Please!" Naturally, Mom and Sis never slowed down, so the yipping would continue as they chased each other around and around, through our woods.

We had only one problem with the three of them. Once in a while, Puzzles would lead the other two off on a merry chase. They would be gone for hours, causing us considerable worry. We enlarged our fenced-in yard, and this was where Leo and Bayley stayed when we were at work or when Puzzles and Crescent joined them on the frequent occasions that they came to visit. We discovered, however, that our Border Collies were good escape artists. In this venture, Leo often assisted them, though he rarely, if ever, ran off with them when they did escape. I think he figured if they left, he could get some peace and quiet. And when Leo did get free, he'd simply lay at the top of our driveway and watch the world go by. Bayley, the first to leave his birthing nest, unfortunately became quite an explorer.

It was Friday, November 22, 1996. Bayley and Crescent were a little over six months old. We were getting ready to attend a retirement party for a colleague of my wife. Amy had brought Puzzles and Crescent to play with Bayley. We put all three Border Collies inside the fence to play. We believed we had it secured. We were wrong. It wasn't too long before they had managed to push under a slight gap in the fence, and all three of them were gone. After an hour or so, Crescent appeared. This was typical. Crescent almost always came back first. Then, typically, after an additional hour or so, Puzzles would appear, with Bayley in tow. This time wasn't typical. Puzzles came back alone. It was nearly dark. Betsy was almost sick with worry.

It was deer hunting season, and she worried aloud that it was a dangerous time for a dog to be on the loose. Deer hunters don't like dogs running around, so her fears were not completely unfounded. We live in the woods, and there are some hunters who seemed to believe posted signs were only put up so that they, the hunters, could rip them down. Still, I tried to reassure my wife.

"Look," I said, "dogs wander off all the time. He's probably okay."

"He's always come back with Puzzles before," she countered.

"I know," I said. "But I'm sure he's okay." I don't think I was very reassuring.

"Why don't we go up over the hill and call?" There is a buried natural gas line that goes through our property that creates a path that goes back from our house. It intersects with another trail about 100 yards behind our house. Puzzles had come back from that direction.

"Okay," Betsy said.

We called for a long time. No response. I'll be honest with you. I was getting worried also. Reluctantly, we made the decision to keep our plans and go to the retirement party. There really didn't seem to be much else to do. Amy had left earlier to go visit a friend. She knew that the dogs had run off but didn't know that only two had returned. We also knew that she would be returning home before us. We got ready, kept Puzzles and Crescent inside (after their adventure, they were ready to sleep the rest of the day and night away), left a note for Amy to call for Bayley when she got home, and went to the retirement dinner.

At dinner, Betsy worried about hunters on our property. Her opinion of hunters, though never very high, had been lowered to considerable depths many years earlier. We had lived in our present location for only three or four years. Betsy returned home from running errands to find a strange car parked in our driveway, about 200 feet from the road. (Remember, our driveway is over 800 feet long.) Since she couldn't get down the driveway, she parked the car at the road and began to walk toward the car. Betsy was a little upset. "Who would park their car so that it blocked someone else's driveway? Not even hunters are that inconsiderate," she thought. She checked the car. It was locked. She decided to wait a while for the car owner to come back. In a moment of naïve romanticism, she wrote a note to car owner.

"To the owner of this car," she began.

"We are more than happy to have you walk in our woods, enjoy the beauty of our stream, and breathe the refreshing fall air," she continued, ever so politely. "Please remember, however, that we do not allow hunting on our property. We have small children and animals that play in these woods.

Thanks,

The Watermans"

She placed the note on the windshield and walked to the house, where she continued to wait for the hunter's return. A steady cold drizzle had been falling most of the day, with temperatures in the low forties. It began to get dark. She vacillated between anger and worry.

"Aren't hunters supposed to stop hunting at dark? How would we know if the hunter had somehow gotten hurt?"

She decided to walk outside to see if she could see anyone. She walked to the top of our driveway and noticed that the car was indeed still there. The car owner hadn't come back from another direction and driven off unnoticed. She also noticed that she was shivering. She went back to the house to get a jacket. Betsy decided it might be a good idea to take Thor, our 120-pound Newfoundland/Setter mix who preceded Leo, with her. Thor, though he looked intimidating, posed no real threat to anyone. He was a gentle giant. Still, he provided a measure of comfort for Betsy as she began looking for the hunter.

Betsy and Thor started down the driveway. As they approached the part of the driveway that stretches from the woods to open meadow, about 500 feet down, Thor suddenly stiffened and looked to the right. Betsy looked over to see a man standing very still, obviously trying to hide. He was just back in the woods, holding a shotgun and smoking. This is not a smart thing to do if you are trying not to be noticed. I'm sure Thor noticed the cigarette odor long before he saw the man.

Any worry that Betsy had for the man's safety was quickly turning to anger. She grabbed Thor's collar, told him to sit, and then pinned his wagging tail to the ground by gently, but firmly, placing her foot on the "feathers" of his tail. What Betsy had was a friendly dog trying to greet a new visitor to our home. What the man saw was a large, pitch black, mean-looking dog straining to attack him. Betsy helped this image by saying, "Easy, Thor. Easy, big boy ..." and making it look like she was using more energy to hold him back than she actually was.

"What are you doing here?" Betsy asked, still using her polite voice.

The man mumbled something unintelligible.

"Do you realize that this is private property and that you're blocking our driveway?" Betsy continued, her anger level rising.

"We didn't see any posted signs," said the man.

"That's because people tear them down. Besides, didn't you notice at some point that this was a private driveway and not a public road?"

Though you can't see our house from the road, it should be obvious after you walk to the top of our driveway that it is *not* a public road, as our house sits at the end of it. Besides, even if it were a public road, it was still blocked.

"I suggest you leave!" Betsy was livid by now.

"I'm waiting for my friends."

It hadn't occurred to Betsy that there was a group of them.

"Just how many of you are there?"

As if on cue, five more men came into view from over the hill.

"C'mon guys, we have to get out of here right now," said the first man.

The combination of my wife and Thor can be pretty intimidating, especially when you know you're in the wrong.

"Do you guys always just park and hunt wherever you want?" Betsy asked incredulously.

Then one of the men, obviously drunk, put his face to hers, took a swig from a bottle he was carrying, and blurted in a drunken slur, "Look, lady, we heard there's a big buck out here, and we're gonna get 'im."

This sent Betsy over the edge. Not backing down one iota, she stepped up, put her face in his, and with more than just a little sarcasm, she said, "If there's a big buck out there, he's obviously a lot smarter than you. He's probably curled up somewhere, nice and dry, while you've been sitting out all day in the cold getting soaked." (And sloshed, I might add.)

Naturally, the man did not take kindly to her words. He leaned in even closer, and retorted with all the intelligent wit he had in him, "Oh yeah?"

The others now started moving toward him.

"C'mon Jim. Get in the car."

His friends, aware that they were face to face with an enraged woman and her killer dog, tried to stuff their mouthy, drunken friend into the car. Betsy's mouth dropped as each began to unload his gun. It had never occurred to her that these men, in various states of inebriation, were still carrying loaded guns, and she was alone with them in an isolated spot. They all got in the car and quickly drove away. Betsy stood watching them leave, shaking her head in disbelief.

But that was a long time ago. Now it was Bayley we were worried about.

❄ ❄ ❄

We arrived at the retirement party a little late. Though very distracted, we managed to do and say all the right things. About 8:30, we were able to make a graceful exit. We headed home.

We were barely on our way when our cell phone rang. When I answered, all I heard was Amy sobbing. Immediately, I thought, *Bayley's dead.*

"Amy, what's the matter?" I asked.

Betsy, who sensed my distress, started asking, "What's happened? Is Bayley all right? I knew something awful happened to him."

"Bayley's been shot," Amy responded, still sobbing. "He's at the vets' right now. I took him as fast as I could."

"Then he's still alive?" I asked.

"Yes," Amy managed.

"Okay. We'll go directly to the vets." As fate would have it, the vets' office was only a few minutes away.

"Bayley's alive, but he has been shot. He's at the vets' now. Amy found him and took him right over," I told Betsy as soon as I hung up with Amy.

"Damn! I knew it! I just knew it. Those damn hunters!" Betsy pounded the steering wheel. "They think they own the f---in' world. Go anywhere, shoot anything they want."

"Betsy, take it easy. Let's get to the vets' in one piece. We don't need to rush. It's only a couple of miles away, and the roads might be a little slippery."

It had snowed just enough that day to cover the ground and make driving a little tricky. And my wife, who does most of the driving, has been known to weigh in on the gas pedal from time to time, though under normal circumstances, she respects the road conditions we have around here. These were not normal circumstances, but she got herself under control, and in about five minutes, we were at the vets'. It was a little after 9 p.m. The staff had all gone home. Dr. O., the vet on call, met us at the door and took us back to where he was treating Bayley. Bayley was already under anesthetic.

"How is he?" we both asked at once.

"He's lost a lot of blood," answered Dr. O. "We took an X-ray, and miraculously, the shooter didn't get any of the bone."

He showed us the wound. It was huge.

"It appears that the bullet went in here," he said, pointing to the front of the rear left hip, "and came out here," pointing to the rear of his left hip. "I don't know how it missed the bone, but it did."

It was the first bit of good news that we'd heard. If the bullet were as little as a quarter-inch closer to his body, the damage might have been catastrophic.

"Why would someone do this? Bayley had to be coming toward the person who shot him," I observed. "He was just trying to be friendly. I mean, look at this. That's the only way it could've happened. And he had to have used a deer slug. The entrance hole is about an inch in diameter, but the exit hole is four inches long."

This meant, of course, that the perpetrator was a hunter. Betsy could contain herself no longer. She, who rarely swears, began to critique all the hunters in the world in very colorful language.

"Stupid damn hunters. F---in' damn hunters. They think they own the whole damn, f---in' world!" She had added some superlatives since the car ride.

She paced the room, occasionally looking over at Bayley, an innocent, six-month-old puppy, whose only sin for this horror was trying to be friendly. Our sin had been in some-how not having a secure enough fence.

Dr. O., in an attempt to calm things down, piped in, "Not all hunters are like that. Once in a while, I go out hunting."

Betsy, who still had some level of self-control, realized that it would do no good to anger the person treating our dog. She sputtered to a stop.

We were there for about an hour. Dr. O. went about methodically cleaning the wound. He estimated that Bayley would lose approximately twenty-five percent of the muscle mass in his hip. The doctor said it was too early to tell what the residual effects would be. We also discussed whether we should report the incident to the State Police.

"I firmly believe that you should report it," said Dr. O.

"What good would it do?" responded Betsy. "There's no way we can prove anything, even if they found somebody."

"I know," said Dr. O., "but at least the police will know that there's somebody around shooting dogs."

"I suppose you're right," Betsy acknowledged.

Dr. O. finished stitching both wounds. He gave us one of those clown collars that are shaped like a cone, showed us how to use it, and told us how important it was that Bayley keep the collar on.

"If you don't keep this on, Bayley will go right after those stitches and pull them out," Dr. O warned.

After a few minutes, Betsy did manage to settle down and turned her energies toward comforting Bayley. I don't want to leave the impression that I was not also angry. It's just that Betsy tends to externalize things, and I tend to internalize them. I guess I let her vent my anger for me.

About an hour after we got there, Bayley started to come around. "It's okay, Bay. You're gonna be all right, boy. We're right here, fella. We're going take you home now."

Bayley looked up at us, confused but happy to see us. He even started to wag his tail. It wasn't much—little more than the tip of his tail rising and falling from the treatment table— but a wag, nonetheless.

"You're going to have to give him these antibiotics, one tablet, twice a day," said Dr. O.

"Okay," we answered.

"If he seems like he's in a lot of pain, you could try giving him half an aspirin. Dogs tolerate aspirin pretty well. On the other hand, with a wound that bad, I would try to hold off for a few days. Aspirin is a blood thinner, and we don't want the wound to start bleeding."

"Right."

"He'll probably still be a little groggy tomorrow. It takes a while for the anesthetic to wear off completely." He continued, sensing our concern, "Overall, he's a young, healthy dog. He's got that going for him. You can call tomorrow and make an appointment for about ten days from now. We'll check him out and remove his stitches then."

"Thanks, Dr. O.," Betsy said as I gathered up Bayley with his new clown collar and we headed toward the door. "I'm sorry I went off like I did. I'm still very upset."

"That's okay. I understand," returned Dr. O.

"Yeah. Thanks," I added.

We got in the car. Having a dog with one of those silly, but necessary, collars made this no small feat. Because of the weather conditions, we had decided to take the Subaru, with its all-wheel drive. It's a nice little car, but it is a tad on the small side. After a very brief discussion, we figured it would be best to lay him on the back seat with me next to him. It's amazing how large that collar becomes when you're trying to get it through a smallish car door.

With Betsy's help, I lowered Bayley onto his right side on the back seat. I went around to the other side of the car and got in next to him. Betsy had gone out earlier to warm up the car so that Bayley wouldn't get cold. We started home. I kept one hand on Bayley, stroking him from time to time. Bayley mostly slept, but occasionally he would half wake up, look up at me, wag his tail just a little, and then fall back to sleep.

When we got home, it was nearly 11 p.m. I carried Bayley into the house and took him directly to the bedroom. Amy was waiting for us.

"How's Bayley?" she asked as we came through the door.

"Not great. He's lost a lot of blood and muscle. The vet said he's lost about twenty-five percent of the muscle in his hip. Luckily, there is no bone damage. Still, it's a really bad wound," Betsy answered.

"Oh, you poor thing," said Amy as she approached Bayley. She was upset, but relieved that Bayley was alive. "How long do you have to wear that silly collar?" Then she turned to us. "How long does he have to wear that silly collar?"

"Don't know. At least until the stitches are out, probably a little longer. It depends on how fast it heals," answered Betsy.

I continued to our bedroom while Betsy and Amy discussed the evening's events. I set Bayley down next to my side of the bed. Leo, who had already put himself to bed, raised his head, looked over, and then lay back down. Bayley fussed a little with the collar but was soon fast asleep. I went back out to the living room. By then, Amy had gathered up Puzzles and Crescent and gone back to her house.

"Let's go to bed," I said.

"I don't know if I can sleep. I'm too worked up."

"I know. Me too."

We went into the bedroom, exhausted, but as predicted, neither of us was able to sleep very much. Too much adrenaline and too much worry about Bayley. I was able to doze off occasionally, but I would wake up, put my hand on Bayley to make sure he was breathing, and then roll back over. Betsy mostly read and plotted what she was going to do the next day. She decided to get up early, bang on some pots and pans to alert the deer, so they could hide from the hunters, and then go hunting for hunters. At 5:30 in the morning, she pulled me out of bed.

"It's still dark outside," I observed. "It won't be light for another hour."

"I know. I want to get out before the hunters and alert the deer." She grabbed some pots and pans while telling me of her plan.

Though barely conscious, I thought of a possible unwanted side effect.

"You know," I said, "it's possible that all we'll do is scare the deer toward the hunters."

She stood stock still. "Oh. You could be right. That's the last thing I want to do." Slowly she began hanging the pots and pans back on the rack. "But I am going out to see if I can find anybody. Are you coming with me?"

"It's dark outside," I reminded her.

"It's starting to get light," she responded.

"Okay." I figured that this was not the time to argue. Besides, the first signs of light were beginning to appear. Our first tack was to drive along Hadley Road and see if there were any cars parked alongside. We found one, but it was quite a way away. Betsy was right. Those guys get out even earlier than I thought. We decided that the people in this car were probably going to be well away from our woods. This doesn't mean that one of them was not the perpetrator, but it would be foolish to go traipsing in unfamiliar woods until it was much lighter. Our second tack was to go to the back of the Oswego County Fairgrounds, which connects with our property and offers easy parking.

"I need to get something to eat." I'm diabetic, and if we were going to be walking around in the woods, I needed to eat. Betsy sometimes finds this a little frustrating, but having a husband going hypoglycemic on her would not be good.

"Okay," she agreed.

I wolfed down a bowl of cold cereal, Betsy drank an instant breakfast, and we were back out the door. We decided to drive around to the back of the fairgrounds to see if anyone was parked over there. The trail that runs behind our house opens onto the back parking lot of the fairgrounds. In fact, when the fair is running, we walk over the hill and take this trail to the fair. Some hunters like to park here so they don't have to park alongside the road. Of course, they can only do this when there isn't much snow. On this day, there was only enough snow to cover the ground—or just enough to track deer.

We drove to the fairgrounds and wound our way to the back parking lot. There it was—a small, brown, four-wheel-drive pickup with a plow blade on the front. As we got out of our car, we noticed a gun rack in the truck's window. This was definitely a hunter's vehicle. I could see that Betsy's anger level was starting to rise again. The weather was gorgeous. The sun had risen to just above the treetops, and the snow glistened. But neither one of us were in the mood to enjoy this beautiful morning. We had a dog-shooter to find.

"Come on," said Betsy. "We should be able to track him."

She was right. There was one set of boot tracks leading from the truck.

"Remember, he's probably armed," I said, stating the obvious.

We discussed our strategy. We could track the person quietly and try to catch him in the act, or we could track the hunter while making noise. We quickly reasoned that it would not be wise to surprise someone with a loaded weapon, so we chose the latter strategy. Better to lose the element of surprise and stay alive. We started down the trail. We'd barely gotten started when a rifle-toting figure headed toward us. We soon recognized who it was.

"I think that's Karl," said Betsy.

"I think you're right."

Karl was a friend who had asked permission to cross our property to hunt in a field that lay adjacent to ours. We gave permission and appreciated that he was able to help us keep an eye on our land during hunting season.

"Anything the matter?" asked Karl as he headed toward us.

"Somebody shot one of our dogs yesterday. We were checking to see if that hunter might just show up on our land today," answered Betsy.

"Somebody shot one of your dogs?"

"Bayley, our six-month-old Border Collie."

"Jeez. Some of the people around here. Makes you wonder, doesn't it?" His voice trailed off as he shook his head. Then he asked, "Could he have been running deer? Or could somebody have mistaken him for a deer?"

"Not likely. At six months he'd make a pretty small deer, and he's black and white. For another, we know from the bullet wound that Bayley was facing directly at the shooter, headed toward the person. It's likely he was just trying to be friendly." Betsy went on to describe the wound and relate the prior evening's events.

"I was out here yesterday morning, but I don't recall seeing anybody." Karl continued, "I can only hunt in the morning, I have to open the restaurant at 11. I was headed back now. And I hunt with a rifle. I don't like using a shotgun. Do you have any idea where he was shot?"

"Not really. We don't think it was too far away. It doesn't seem he could've have dragged himself very far."

"If I get a chance, I'll look around. See if I can see anything."

We decided to go back to the house. It was obvious that Karl was the only person near our property on this morning. We got back in the car and went home. When we got home, we were hit by another shock. Now that it was light out, we could see how much Bayley had struggled. Blood stains on the front porch. Blood stains on the back deck, by both the dining room door and our bedroom door.

Bayley had struggled home, dragged himself from door to door trying to find someone, and we were off partying. We already felt guilty that we had not kept him safely in his fence, and now we felt doubly so. It reminded us again of just how badly hurt he was. It also showed us what a gutsy little guy he was. I think just about everybody has heard that Borders are "the smartest dogs." Not so many know just how courageous and how much heart they have. Bayley had needed every bit of it.

About an hour after we got back to the house, we heard a knock on our door. It was Karl.

"Hi. We didn't expect to see you again so soon," said a surprised Betsy.

"I figured I had some time, so I went back to see if could pick up a trail. I found a pool of blood back off the trail a little."

"Could you tell if it was on our property?" I asked.

"Yeah, I think so. You go as far as the power lines and back to the stone fence, don't you?"

"Yes," I answered.

"Then whoever shot your dog wasn't where he was supposed to be. It's back near that corner where the power lines cross the fence." He continued, "I don't get it. You don't allow anybody to hunt back here but me, do you?"

Neither my wife nor I had remembered giving him permission to actually hunt on our land, but now was not the time to bring it up. "The same with Pratt" (our neighbor to the east who owns the strip of land between us and the fairgrounds). "And I don't think Jess lets anybody hunt on his property but his boys." (Jess was our neighbor to the back.) All the lands around you are posted. I can't imagine any of them doing anything like this," Karl said.

Frankly, neither could we. We knew Jess's boys. They were all adults now. The oldest had dated our older foster daughter for a brief time. The middle one had been a friend of our foster son. A memory of Mike, the middle son, sprung to mind. We had gone to their farm for some reason I can't recall. It might have been to get some maple syrup. I think Jess was still running his sugar bush then. Anyway, we were getting ready to leave when Mike, the middle son, came running out to the car. The next thing you know, he's looking under it.

"One of the kittens likes to lay underneath cars. I just wanted to make sure you didn't run over him," he said it with a tenderness that surprised us. Mike was a wrestler, a tough guy. This particular action belied his image. These were farm cats, after all. Kittens were a dime a dozen. The fact that he even noticed this behavior was quite remarkable and revealed to us the true nature of this seemingly tough kid.

"Thanks, Karl, for doing this," I said. "We really appreciate it."

"If I get a chance, I'll try putting up some posted signs again. At least they won't be able to say 'Gee, there weren't any posted signs.'"

"Good luck. We put them up, and they just take them down," said Betsy.

"I know," answered Karl, "but maybe it'll slow them up. You never know."

"True," I said.

"I wish I could find the guy who did this. I wonder how he'd like to be shot. Well, I gotta get going, or I'm gonna be late. At least they can't fire me," said Karl, who owned his own restaurant, as he headed toward the door.

It was a good thing Karl came along. He did make us realize that not all hunters are irresponsible, drunken slugs. The vast majority are good citizens. The problem is that the few who aren't are carrying knives and loaded rifles.

After Karl left, we discussed whether we should call the police. We decided we should. We didn't think it would do much good, but it seemed like the right thing to do. And our vet had been pretty clear that he felt the police should be notified. The officer showed up about 11 a.m. I had been running some errands. He was already there sitting on the sofa when I walked into the house. He introduced himself:

"Hello. I'm Officer Johnson."

Even when they're on your side, I'm a little intimidated by police officers. And here one sat on my couch, wearing his bulletproof vest, gun in his holster, listening to our story.

"Your wife told me what happened," he said. Then he became more agitated. "Let me tell you, I'd be pretty upset if somebody shot my dog."

"What kind of dog do you have?" we asked.

"A nine-month-old German Shepherd. He rides all over with me in my pickup. He's just like one of my own kids." Good, we got a dog person.

"Isn't it illegal to shoot a dog, even if they're running deer?" I asked.

"It sure is. It's illegal to shoot a dog for any reason." He resumed his professional demeanor. "I'll ask around. You realize that I probably won't be able to find the person that shot your dog."

"We know that."

"If I do find anything, I'll let you know." He then became agitated again. "I wish I could find him."

We didn't really expect anything to come of all this. We had done our duty, and now it was time for the process of healing to begin. Not just Bayley, though he certainly was by far the most urgent. We had to get over our feelings of anger and guilt. They were destructive emotions and did little to change anything. Instead, we knew we needed to do a better job of keeping Bayley close to home.

We stopped by the fairgrounds on our way back from the store. We were pleasantly surprised to see that Karl had already made good on his promise. There were copious posted signs all along the fairground's boundary. If someone were to try to take down all the signs, it would take them a good, long time. Hopefully, it wouldn't be worth the effort, and they would just go hunt somewhere else.

We also discovered that Officer Johnson had made good on his promise to "ask around." As we talked to our neighbors over the following weeks, we learned that he had gone house to house, asking if anyone had seen anything. Our faith in humanity was being restored. There are lots of good people out there. As predicted, though, we never found out who shot Bayley. And we know we never will. Still, the posted signs don't come down as much or as fast as they used to.

As for Bayley, the healing process went well. He had some problems with his clown collar, primarily knocking it into the door jambs around the house. He also occasionally ran into *us*. Not fun, but in about six weeks, he was able to go without the collar. One problem that outlived the presence of the collar was that he had trouble having a bowel movement. He could no longer use the injured leg to balance himself.

When he took the position, his hind leg seemed to naturally curl up. He quickly learned to do a three-legged poop, and he continued that stance all his life.

In the meantime, we inadvertently trained Bayley to suspect all snacks. In an effort to get him to take his antibiotic, we tried to disguise it by putting it in various treats. We tried cheese, hot dogs, cheese curls, steak, all kinds of doggie treats, and probably some others. Not only did it not work, but now Bayley was always suspicious and proceeded very cautiously when taking snacks from us. And I had to resort to the "stuff it down the throat" method, which neither of us liked at all.

We had a fair amount of snow that winter. This is always a concern in terms of fencing. The more snow that piles up, the shorter the fence becomes. By the end of December, the snow began to accumulate in serious amounts. Bayley was pretty much healed. We frequently took him along cross-country skiing with us. Leo went along too, and pretended to pull, but Betsy did most of the skiing herself that winter, simply happy to have her two dogs trotting along with her. Betsy quietly decided that skiing under her own power wouldn't be that bad. It was good exercise, after all.

Chapter 3

Oh No! Not Again!

The winter was slowly losing its grip on Sandy Creek. The beginning of April still saw snow, but it was disappearing. By mid-April, there were only patches of snow and ice left. It's a transition month. One day, warm and sunny, T-shirt weather. The next, cold and dreary, winter-coat weather. This Friday in April was one of the cold, dreary days. To make matters worse, there was a half drizzle/half rain falling—a good day to be inside. Amy, Puzzles, and Crescent were visiting us for the weekend. We put all the dogs in the fenced yard. We had shored up the fence, we thought. By midafternoon, though, the Borders had managed to escape yet again. As usual, Crescent reappeared first, then Puzzles. Where was Bayley?

It wasn't hunting season, so it didn't seem likely he could have been shot. But the same scenario as last fall was playing itself out again. This time we didn't have any obligations for the evening. We put on our jackets and went looking. It was early evening, but there was still light. We walked around our trail, calling. Nothing. We walked back over the hill and into Jess's woods. Nothing. We got in the car and drove up and down our road. Nothing. We drove around the fairgrounds. Nothing. We were getting that sinking feeling. Panic, really, and disbelief. How could we have let it happen again?

We should have control over this. How could we have let it happen *again*?

"Look, Bets, it's not hunting season. He's just wandered off," I said as we headed back home from the fairgrounds. "He's probably home now, waiting for us."

"I hope you're right, but I have a sickening feeling."

"I know," I said.

We pulled in the driveway and walked in the door.

"No Bayley yet," said Amy. "I'm getting really worried about him."

"So are we."

"What if he has been hit by a car, and dragged himself off somewhere?" I said.

We watched TV, mostly to distract us. Every fifteen to twenty minutes one of us would get up and call outside. We were getting very discouraged. Finally, about midnight, we went to bed. I fell into a fitful sleep. Sometime in the middle of the night, I woke up. I decided to check the dog pen. I walked sleepy-eyed out on the deck and to the pen, which opens off the opposite end of the deck from our bedroom. In spite of the fact that it was cold and rainy, I hadn't bothered to put on any clothes. I looked to the gate. I saw two Border Collie heads staring back at me. Then it struck me. One of those had to be Bayley. Amy takes her two dogs to bed with her, but Crescent almost always gets up around midnight and asks to go out. Crescent has this strange behavior. She picks a corner of the pen and declares it her own. When she first goes out, she runs to the corner, barking in case someone or something is there, and takes a defensive posture. Her behavior is near fanatical, earning her the nickname "Psycho Dog." Anyway, back to our story.

"Betsy!" I called. "Bayley's here!"

I leaned over and helped him onto the deck and into the dining room.

"Is he all right?" asked Betsy.

"His right front leg is hurt. He looks like he's been hit by a car."

By now, Betsy had thrown on a robe and come out to help. We could see that his leg was badly damaged.

"Can you call the vet while I get something on?" I asked Betsy.

"Sure," she answered. She called and got an answering service. While I got dressed, Betsy comforted Bayley.

Amy heard the disturbance and called out, "Is Bayley okay?"

"No," answered Betsy. "It looks like he's been hit by a car. His front leg is pretty smashed up. I'm waiting for the vet to call back."

I quickly threw on some jeans and a shirt and switched places with Betsy.

"Nobody's called back yet," Betsy said as I took over the comforting role.

There wasn't any bleeding, but there was considerable tenderness.

"I'm so sorry, Bay. You don't deserve this, do you, fella? You'll be okay, Bay, you'll be okay," I said, over and over. He was in a lot of pain.

The vet called back while Betsy was getting ready. She picked up the phone in the bedroom as she continued to put more clothes on.

"What appears to be the problem?" asked the vet. It was Dr. W.

"We think Bayley, our Border Collie, has been hit by a car," answered Betsy. "It's his right front leg. We think it's broken. It's very tender to the touch."

"You'd better bring him down so I can take a look at it."

"Okay. We'll be there in about ten minutes."

We carefully wrapped Bayley in a towel and set him gently in the back of the car. Dr. W. was waiting for us. He let us in and led us back to one of the examination rooms. He carefully started to examine the leg. The entire leg was tender, but it was obvious that some spots were worse than others. He checked the rest of Bayley to make sure that there weren't any other injuries, especially internal bleeding. There didn't appear to be any. His injuries seemed confined to his leg.

"I won't be able to X-ray his leg until morning. That's when the X-ray tech comes in. You may as well go home." He paused, then continued, "I'll call as soon as we know something."

"Thanks, Dr. W. We appreciate your coming in at this hour." It was about four o'clock in the morning by now.

"Occupational hazard," he responded with a little smile on his face.

We got in our car and headed home without our dog.

"Stupid dogs. Why can't they stay home? Why do they have to run off like that?" asked Betsy, shaking her head sadly.

"It's Puzzles's fault," I added. "She gets loose and takes her kids off to who knows where. Bayley never wanders very far when he's alone." He had not even tried to escape from the fence in months.

Conversations at four in the morning tend not to be very rational.

"No," Betsy said, regaining her rationality. "This is our fault. We have to find a way to secure that fence. Even when Puzzles does come to visit."

"You're right," I admitted. "I'll go out after breakfast and see if I can see where they got out and try to fix it."

Amy heard us as we entered the house.

"How's Bayley?" she called out from her bedroom.

"We don't know for sure yet," I answered. "The vet's going to take X-rays in the morning. The good news is that he doesn't appear to have any internal injuries."

"He's going to call us as soon as he knows something definite. Go back to sleep," Betsy suggested.

"Okay," responded Amy as she drifted back to sleep.

We went to bed also, but we didn't sleep much. We were both too worried about Bayley. We got up early, even though we both knew the vets' office didn't open until nine. On the other hand, we weren't really sleeping, either. I ate breakfast and went outside to see if I could find where the dogs had gotten out. I found a spot where they had moved what I considered large rocks and dug under the fence. I worked to fill the hole and then laid wire along the bottom, covering it with dirt. It was after nine by the time I got back in the house.

"Have you heard anything yet?" I asked as I entered the house. That was kind of a stupid question. If Betsy had heard something, she certainly would have let me know immediately.

"No," she answered.

Finally, a little after ten, the vet called. Betsy took the call. All of a sudden, her expression turned to one of mild horror and disbelief.

"What's wrong?" I asked, knowing I was not going to like her answer.

"Bayley's been shot again!"

For a couple of minutes, I practically went comatose. I couldn't believe it. How could this happen? A ton of emotions ran through me. Anger, guilt, shame, pity, sadness. We had lived here for twenty-five years and never had anything even close to this happen to one of our dogs.

What kind of people live around here, anyway? I asked myself.

We later learned there had been two other dogs shot on our road, and each had died. But we didn't know that then. Betsy finished her conversation with the vet.

"What'd he say?"

"His leg is really bad," Betsy responded. "He thinks it'll have to be amputated. I'm not sure I can deal with that. I know people say that dogs can get along just fine with three legs. It's me. I just don't know if I can deal with it. He's been through so much already, maybe we should just put him down."

"I'm not sure I'm ready to do that," I said. "How's he doing now?"

"Okay, I guess. He's pretty much been sleeping except when they did the X-ray."

"That must've hurt," I said. Anyone who has had an X-ray of a broken bone knows it's not a particularly pleasant experience.

"We mostly talked about what we should do," Betsy continued. "He said he's going to talk to Dr. O. He's their orthopedic vet. Dr. W. said he's not very optimistic, though."

"Well," I said, "we'll see what he has to say before we make any rash decisions."

We went about doing some tedious household chores, waiting for Dr. O. to call. Sometime between one and two in the afternoon, he called. He apparently didn't know that

Dr. W. had already told us Bayley had been shot. When Betsy answered, he was very tentative, remembering Betsy's reaction the first time Bayley had been shot.

"I'm afraid Bayley's been shot again," he said.

"I know," said Betsy. "Dr. W. called this morning and told us."

There seemed to be some relief on Dr. O.'s part.

Betsy continued, "Can we save his leg?"

"Why don't you come down to the office and I can show you the X-rays? Then we can discuss it."

"Do you want us to come right now?" Betsy asked.

"Yes. We have got to move on this soon."

We got in the car and hurried once more to the vets' office. It was Saturday, and past normal working hours, although almost everyone was still there. We waited only a minute or two before we were led into the exam room. Dr. O. entered, carrying Bayley's X-rays. He put them up on the viewer. I was not prepared for what I saw. Both the tibia and the fibula, the two bones that make up the lower leg, were shattered. There were several large segments, and a lot of small pieces. I personally didn't know how the leg could be saved. Then again, I'm not a doctor. Dr. O. started to explain the options.

"We could amputate the leg. Dogs get along just fine on three legs."

"I just don't think I can handle that," Betsy reiterated. "I'm not proud of it, but I just don't think I can." She kept the rest of her thought to herself.

"Now, the other thing I could try is lining up the large bone fragments and hope they fuse together. I have done it before, and it has worked. Bayley's a young, healthy dog, otherwise. He probably has a good chance. They would have to be held in place by pins from the outside. The small bone fragments would eventually be absorbed into the system. The only problem is that it would take at least twelve weeks to heal, and he would have to be kept quiet. That's not easy to do with a young dog."

We stared at the X-rays without saying anything.

Finally, I asked, "Could we talk about this for a few minutes?"

"Sure. Take your time." Dr. O. left the room.

"I think we should have him put down," Betsy said. "It's not right to put him through this all over again. And this time it sounds like it'll be a lot worse. Twelve weeks is a long time." Betsy was highly stressed and seemed on the verge of losing it. She loved Bayley, and the thought of putting him down was not easy for her to take. I knew she was highly conflicted.

She made a strong argument. The healing process would be long and painful. "But Betsy," I said, "He worked so incredibly hard to get back to us. Now we're just gonna say, 'Too bad for you, Bay'? He's young. He's a fighter. It's only twelve weeks. I think we should at least give him a chance."

Betsy didn't respond. I could tell she was thinking about what to do, and it was not easy. After a couple of moments, she spoke, softly and deliberately. "It's just not fair. He's just been through so much, and he's only eleven months old."

"If you think we should put him down, you're going have to tell him. I can't, but I will support you." I was not trying to be mean or put her on the spot. I knew that I would never be able to get the words out. Dr. O. reentered the room.

Betsy motioned toward the X-rays with her hand. "We'll try the pin thing," she said.

I was a little surprised—and relieved.

"Okay," said Dr. O. "We'll get started on the surgery as soon as possible. I'll give you a call when we're done, and let you know when you can take him home."

On the way home, I turned to Betsy and asked quietly, "What made you change your mind?"

"I couldn't say it. I couldn't say 'Put him down.'" She paused for a moment, then asked, "Did we do the right thing?"

"I don't know. How can you know in something like this?"

We went home and waited for the call. We knew if anyone could save Bayley's leg, it was Dr. O. He's a very talented orthopedic veterinarian. We also knew that he was dealing with a very, very bad injury. We waited. Dr. O. called.

"Bayley came through the surgery pretty well. Can you pick him tomorrow?" he asked.

"Okay."

Bayley was asleep when we got there, and we both seemed to begin to breathe again. The bandage on his leg seemed huge. I hadn't realized the pins stuck out as far as they did and had to be bandaged, as well as the leg. He also had been fitted with another clown collar. This one was clear. Bayley was to like this one much better. The clear collar allowed him to see peripherally. We stroked him. Gradually, Bayley came around.

"Like I said, you'll have to keep him quiet," said Dr. O. "And you'll have to bring him in every two weeks to change his bandages and so we can check on his progress and to make sure there's no infection. You also have to keep the bandage dry. If you have a crate, that is probably the best idea."

From a purely physical point of view, keeping him in a crate would indeed probably be the best to keep him quiet. But how do you tell a highly active Border Collie that he has to stay in doggie prison for three months, and that it's for his own good? We ditched the crate idea quickly. We feared it might kill his spirit, and to kill his spirit would be the same as killing him. We would do the best we could at keeping him calm and keeping his bandage dry, but we were also determined to let him live, at least a little bit. As it turned out, this was not an easy thing to do.

As the healing process dragged on, two things became apparent. A flea in Antarctica had a better chance of surviving than us making it through two weeks without a bandage change. The first day went very well. Bayley had been doped up enough so that it was not hard to maintain a quiet household. By the second day, he was feeling better, so we decided to give him a few minutes without his clown collar. We turned our backs for a few minutes and, when we turned around, he was carefully lifting each layer of his bandage off. And so, after only two days, it was back to the vets' for a bandage change. Not a very auspicious start.

"I'm afraid Bayley has managed to undo part of his bandage," I confessed.

"Bring him down and we'll redo it," responded the receptionist. "We'll squeeze him in."

We took him down, bandage dragging. We didn't realize it then, but this was to become an all-too-familiar pattern.

"I know it's hard, but you really do have to keep him quiet," said the vet on call.

She checked his leg. All the time, Bayley seemed to accept his fate with a quiet reserve. We could tell it was hurting him, but he never complained. Occasionally, when the vet touched a particularly tender area, he would flinch, but that was all. He would look at us with those sad eyes as if to say, "Mom and Dad," (he always referred to us as Mom and Dad), "this really hurts, but I'll be okay. Honest. Do you think you could scratch my ears and rub my head?" We both reached over and scratched his ears and rubbed his head. As we did, he lifted his head and gently licked our hands, a little thank-you kiss.

This was the first time we got a good look at the pins. There were four pins going into his leg at right angles, protruding from each side. These were held in place by long vertical pins going down most of the full length of his leg. I wondered if they were trying to make him into some kind of a "borg" dog. No wonder the bandage was so massive.

When she finished, we lifted Bayley from the table and set him on the floor. He went right to the door and waited. He had been good, but now it was time to leave this place. We promised we would try to watch him more carefully.

Bayley with his bandage

And we did try. The next visit wasn't for seven days. We got the same lecture and made the same promise. We also considered keeping him in a crate. No. Every ounce of our bodies felt it was a fundamentally wrong thing to do. So we continued our struggle to maintain a balance between keeping him quiet and letting him live the life of a young dog.

It became harder and harder to keep him down. Our original plan was to keep him in the house and take him out only when he had to go to the bathroom. That worked for about three days. We encountered several problems with this plan. Number one, "when ya gotta go, ya gotta go." This meant taking him out in the rain when necessary, which meant getting the bandage wet. Even on sunny days, it could be a problem. We live in a small clearing in the woods, which, because of the extra shade, means that frequently the dew lasts well into the late morning. Wet grass, wet bandage. We tried wrapping it with a plastic bag. Bayley figured that one out after five minutes.

Even in the house, Bayley wouldn't just lie there. He was still a pup, after all. He would get a toy from his toy box and throw it in the air, gleefully bouncing back and forth. He soon learned to throw the toy in the air, catch it in his clown collar, and dump it on the floor. He would do this over and over. This was not exactly keeping him quiet, but it was darn cute. And at least he wasn't moving around much.

Next, we started taking him on short walks. Running was out of the question; the vet made that very clear—but, unfortunately, not to Bayley. Although Bayley had been to obedience school and had learned leash respect, he simply had too much energy to not pull. And this was not the time to yank back on his leash to remind him. Nonetheless, it was either walks or nothing. Our favorite place to walk was back over the hill. The grass is much longer through much of the first part of the trail, which means wet grass, which means … Well, you get the picture. One time we managed to get Bayley back to our yard relatively dry. We were feeling pretty darn smug. We had succeeded. Then, just as we got back in our yard, we had a mental lapse and Bayley, ever the opportunist, jumped into our large garden pond as we walked him too close. When will we learn?

The second thing that became apparent was that the twelve weeks given for healing was highly optimistic. Four months went by … then five … then six. Dealing with those damn bandages was an ongoing challenge. We never came close to keeping the bandage on for two weeks at a time. We'd soften under Bayley's pleading looks and take off his clown collar for a short break. We'd get distracted and then look down to find that Bayley was carefully unrolling the bandage. He got quite good at this. After Betsy and I got through the blaming routine ("I thought you were watching him." "No, you were supposed to be."), we would determine whose turn it was to call the vets' office and confess that, once again, Bayley needed a new bandage.

One day, he escaped from the house. He went tearing up over the hill, his broken leg dangling in the air. This was not an easy feat. Between the pins and the bandages, his leg was much heavier and bulkier than normal, yet it barely seemed to slow him down. Bayley became quite proficient at moving about with his bad leg. He would hold it up and out to the side. After several heart-stopping minutes, he came back smiling, muddy, and his bandage soaking wet. After our relief, we both shook our heads, somewhat dejectedly. Back to the vet again. Once we made it ten days, but I think the average was closer to four or five days. The shortest time was *one day*.

In embarrassment, we decided that we would try to bandage the leg ourselves. We ended up going to three drug stores to get the combination of bandage materials we figured we needed.

We had expected that twelve weeks would be the end of all of our bandage worries. We were wrong. That first twelve weeks went very slowly. At one month, they did another X-ray. The bones had indeed started to fuse, but the bonds were still very weak. Dr. O.'s plan seemed to be working, but not at the pace we had all hoped. Finally, in mid-July, we took Bayley back to the vets' for what we thought was his last visit. Dr. O. met us in the examination room. I was overly optimistic.

"Bayley, you should get those nasty pins taken out today. Won't that be great?"

"Bayley, let's see how that leg is doing," said the vet. Then he turned to us, "I hear he's been back a few times to get his leg redone."

"Yes," we admitted, a little chagrined. "We try to keep him quiet, but it's not easy. He seems to find ways to get that thing messed up."

"Let's take a picture of that leg and see what's up."

Dr. O. disappeared with Bayley to the back area where they do the X-rays and surgeries. After a few moments he reappeared, carrying several X-rays. They included the original, the one taken at one month, and the current one, at three months. When I saw them, my heart fell.

"It doesn't seem that enough healing has taken place to take out the pins yet," explained Dr. O.

In fact, it didn't look much different than the one-month X-ray. We both were very discouraged. Three months of hope were quickly dashed.

"Come back in about four weeks, and we'll see how he's doing then."

"Thanks, Dr. O.," Betsy said. "Do you still think this will work?"

"Remember, I said it would take *at least* 12 weeks. I certainly wouldn't give up yet. Just—"

We finished his sentence: "Try to keep him quiet." All the vets seem to think a dog's energy was like a volume control we can just turn up or down. It simply was not that easy. We were talking about a very young, energetic dog.

Bayley quickly became the sweetheart of the vets' office. All the techs, all the receptionists couldn't get over the fact that, no matter how many times we had to bring him back, Bayley would never act afraid and was always very cooperative. When we brought him, bandage missing, they would always say something like, "Oh no, Bayley. Not again. You're such a brave little guy."

The vets were sometimes frustrated with us, but always patient with Bayley. We would always get the "You must keep him quiet" lecture, and we always promised to do a better job. One vet even threatened that they would have to start charging us for materials. When he saw our dejected faces, he backed off a little. We just couldn't bring ourselves to shut Bayley off from the world to protect his bandage. We wanted him to have his spirit left at the end of all this.

He was a brave little guy. Only once, during his months-long ordeal, did he make any sound, and when he did, it was horrifying. We had gone for ice cream at the local ice cream place. Bayley and Leo were in the car. Suddenly we heard one of the most dreadful, high shrieking cries we had ever heard coming from our car. We went running over.

Betsy got there first. Bayley was stiff and his back was arched.

"I think he's having convulsions."

I ran over to the other side of the car and opened the door nearest Bayley.

"Can you see anything?" Betsy asked, panic in her voice.

"No," I answered.

Bayley continued to scream. We could both see the extreme terror on his face.

"Wait a minute. I think one of his pins is caught on the seat."

One of his pins had poked through at the bottom and ripped through the fabric of the seat. It was not a clean hole. The pin had kind of woven itself into the seat cover. In what seemed like hours, but was only a few seconds, I managed to free him. All of us, including Bayley, breathed a big sigh of relief. We both sat there with him, comforting him. In the meantime, Leo had jumped to the back of the station wagon, looking concerned but realizing that he was better off out of the way. In a few minutes, Bayley relaxed. Then we relaxed. We went over to the ice cream window. The girl behind the counter inquired about Bayley.

"Is everything all right?"

"Yeah. He's okay, but it was pretty scary, and he clearly was in a lot of pain," Betsy answered.

"Here, maybe this will make him feel better." The girl at the window handed Betsy a small ice cream cone, complete with a few dog biscuits.

"Thanks." Betsy took ice cream and biscuits and gave them to Bayley and Leo. I got a small soft twist and Betsy got a small maple walnut. As usual, I saved the last few bites for Leo, and Betsy saved her last few bites for Bayley.

Everything was almost back to normal. But it had been a very traumatic experience for us all.

That was far and away the worst incident during his healing process. It is hard to describe in words just how awful his scream had sounded. Like something out of this world, and it reminded us of just how fragile his leg was. The injury had occurred toward the beginning of the summer. It was now nearing the middle of November, and the X-ray at month six had shown little progress. We were becoming very discouraged. How long do we let this thing go on, anyway? Seven months? Eight? We had already made plans to visit our daughter Shelley and her husband Thom for a combined Thanksgiving/Christmas celebration at their home in Houston. We arranged for a friend to take care of Bayley some time before, expecting that by now the pins would be gone. Leo had died that September. The pins were not gone, though, and there was no reason to believe that they would be. We took Bayley in for his seven-month checkup. It was just one day before we were scheduled to fly to Houston. Dr. O. happened to be the vet on duty that day.

"Bayley, back again, I see."

"Dr. O., do you think that there's really any hope that he's going to get better?" Betsy asked.

"Well, let's take a picture of it and see how he's doing."

He once again gently lifted Bayley and took him into the back. He seemed to be taking longer than usual. He reappeared, leading Bayley on a leash. No bandages, no pins. *What's going on here?*

"His leg is much better," said Dr. O. He put the X-rays up of six months and the one he had just taken. I couldn't believe my eyes. In one month's time, his leg had seemed to have miraculously healed.

"I don't understand. Why did this suddenly heal?"

"It was probably healing more than it appeared. But sometimes this type of thing does happen. The healing process goes slowly for a while and then for some reason, goes quickly. That's why I didn't want to give up."

"This is great. We were beginning to think it would never happen," I said.

Betsy and I could hardly contain our joy and surprise. No more embarrassing trips to the vets'. No more trying to keep him quiet (except for the next few days). Most important of all, though, Bayley had his leg back. He was a full-fledged dog. We knew that there was still healing that had to take place, that his leg might never be full strength, and that there might be arthritic pain from time to time as he aged, but the worst was over. We felt like celebrating. Yippee!

"You'll still need to keep him quiet for a few days."

'Keep him quiet'—a phrase we'd learned to hate.

"Oh dear," Betsy said. "We're supposed to fly to Houston tomorrow." She said that as much to me as to the vet.

"Laurie will take wonderful care of him," I reassured her.

"How long are you going to be gone?" asked Dr. O.

"Six days."

"I think you should kennel him. There's a very good kennel not too far from here. A person who used to work here as a vet tech runs it. And I want to put him on some antibiotics until the pin holes close up completely."

I turned to Betsy. "Laurie will do a super job and is really looking forward to taking care of him."

While Laurie had never actually met Bayley, from our numerous conversations at work, she felt like she knew him. She really did want to take care of him. Now, except for the meds, it would be a little easier. We took down the name of the kennel, but we knew that Laurie was our first choice.

We called Laurie as soon as we got home. She was thrilled to hear Bayley's good news.

"Of course, I'll still take care of him." She almost acted insulted that we would even ask. "I've bought him a few new toys to play with. I can hardly wait to have him here."

That was the response I expected. That's why I wasn't hesitating to leave Bayley with her.

"We'll drop him off tomorrow morning on our way to the airport," Betsy confirmed. "It'll be some time around nine."

We arrived at her townhouse a little after 9 a.m. Running a little late seems to be part of our normal pattern. Laurie was anxiously waiting for us.

"Sorry we're late."

"Oh, that's okay. And this must be Bayley. Hi, Bayley. How ya doin,' fella?"

As she said this, Bayley leaped up on her, reaching his face up to give her a little kiss. This is a habit we still have not managed to break. I'm afraid our hearts just aren't into it.

"You're not going to be late for your plane, are you?" I think she wanted us to get going so she could start playing with Bayley. "I went out and bought the food that you said you feed him. Do you have the medicine I need to give him? How often does he get these pills? And I need to keep him a little quiet, right?"

"Right, and he gets two pills a day," Betsy answered. "He doesn't take the pills willingly, so that may be a bit of a struggle."

"Oh, that's okay. We'll manage."

We exchanged phone numbers and encouraged each other to call to get or give updates on how Bayley was doing.

We headed for our car, and Laurie led Bayley into her town-house. He looked back at us, a little confused, but being the friendly and cooperative dog that he is, he followed her willingly. It didn't hurt that she also had some really good dog treats with her. A woman with doggie treats can't be all bad.

"Do you think he'll be all right?" Betsy asked me.

"Laurie will be great with him. She'll probably spoil him rotten, and he won't want to come home with us."

"You're right. I just worry about his leg." We had become so accustomed to having the pins in his legs, that we were unsure what this new phase in his healing might bring.

"I know," I said. "But I think he'll be fine."

The flight to Houston was uneventful. We arrived mid-Tuesday afternoon before Thanksgiving. We both worried about Bayley. We celebrated a traditional Thanksgiving on Thursday with our daughter and her family and, as was our tradition on these visits, were preparing on Friday morning to celebrate Christmas later that day, when Laurie called.

"This is Laurie. I hope I'm not interrupting anything."

"No, no. Of course not. How's Bayley doing?" Betsy asked.

"He's doing great. He sleeps with me on my waterbed. He loves the little toys I got him. We're having a great time."

Sleeping with her on her waterbed? He may never want to come home, we thought.

"His leg seems to be doing really well. I take him on walks every morning and afternoon. I really am enjoying him being here." It crossed my mind that this might have been the type of owner who actually could have kept an injured puppy quiet. Who wouldn't have had to take him back every few days for a bandage change.

Betsy and Laurie continued to chat for a few more minutes. The call made us feel a bit relieved, but it also made us realize that we missed the little guy. His horrible seven- month ordeal was behind him. His leg would continue to bother him from time to time, but the worst was over. He was a healthy dog again.

In retrospect, though, we still wonder if it was fair to make him go through all of that. He was only sixteen months old. Nine of those had been spent recovering from gunshot wounds. Yet he never complained. He faced each day with all the Border Collie heart and courage he had, and then some. Also, I didn't know it then, but he would inspire me in my own prolonged illness later on. But that's another story for a later time.

We picked up Bayley on our way home from the airport late Sunday afternoon. Laurie and Bayley were waiting for us. Laurie was clearly sad to see him go. He had a way of capturing your heart.

"Here is his toy that he loves, and here are the treats that he loves," Laurie said as she handed me his leash. "I'm gonna miss him awfully. We've had such a good time." Then she turned to Bayley and said, "Bayley, you're the world's best dog!"

No argument there.

Chapter 4

We Need Another Dog

We arrived home late Sunday afternoon, the first Sunday in December. It's always good to get home, but this was especially good. It hadn't really sunk in that Bayley was almost back to normal. We could look at him and not see huge pins protruding from the bandages. Our long battle of trying to keep him quiet was over. No more bandage battles. No more stuffing-antibiotic-pills-down-his-neck battles. What were we to do with all of our spare time? It was a dilemma we welcomed.

As for Bayley, he was happy to be home, too. Though he clearly enjoyed his visit with Laurie, especially his extended sleeps on her waterbed, he was home with Mom and Dad, and life was as it should be. He did go into the bedroom, once or twice, look at our bed, and communicate that we really should get a waterbed. He seemed to be saying, "Border Collies sleep best on a waterbed."

It's a good thing Bayley healed when he did. The holiday season was upon us. Still, overriding all the holiday stuff was the question, "What are we going to do about cross-country skiing and skijoring?" In anticipation of the winter season, we had recently purchased the belt, tug line, and harness for Bayley and Betsy. We knew that Bayley wouldn't be strong enough to pull Betsy by himself like Leo had done, but Betsy thought that if she really worked, she could help him enough that it would not stress his weakened leg. Me skiing alone, Betsy and Bayley helping one another, perhaps we could ski together.

At the same time, we discussed the possibility that another dog might be needed. Besides, part of us just wanted another dog, but Betsy had reverted to the "one dog is enough" mentality. Now that all of our children were gone, I felt like the house was kind of empty. We talked about getting an Alaskan Malamute. Big and strong, it would barely notice that Betsy was behind it. For the time being, though, Bayley was all the dog we needed.

We thought we might need to upgrade some of our equipment. With this in mind, we attended a local ski fair. It was the first full weekend in December. The Tug Hill Ski Club sponsors this event. People bring their used cross-country ski equipment to sell. Sometimes a retailer will bring some other items like waxes, boots, snowshoes, and poles, though rarely do you see brand-new skis. We were there milling around when a musher couple, Art and Karen, showed up with two of their Siberian Huskies. They were currently training to race in the Iditarod in Alaska. We mentioned that we might be getting a Malamute for skijoring.

"You don't want a Malamute," Art asserted.

How does he know what we want? I thought.

"One of these Huskies would pull you as far and as fast as you'd want to go. You don't need a dog any bigger than this," he said pointing to one of his Huskies.

"Really?" I said looking at them with a little skepticism. He didn't know my wife and her love for speed.

"Oh yeah. No problem. A Malamute, I'm afraid, would be more dog than your wife would want to handle. They're big and strong, all right, but they can also be a little stubborn and thick-headed. They are also a lot slower that a Husky."

We weren't sure we agreed with his assessment, but he wasn't asking our opinion.

"So, one of those Huskies would have no trouble pulling me?" Betsy asked, seeming at least a little interested.

"Nope."

"How about that? They look so small."

Remember, we had had a Belgian Sheepdog most recently (other than Bayley, of course, who we expected to be small) and a Newfoundland before that. Anything under seventy-five pounds looked like a lap dog to us.

"They're a lot stronger than you think," Karen assured us.

We were still a little skeptical. The two Huskies they had with them looked not much bigger than Bayley.

Just then a local high school teacher and avid cross-country skier, who had heard our conversation, chipped in.

"I know someone who has Husky puppies for sale."

"Oh really. Who?"

"She's one of my former students. She lives up near Mannsville with her boyfriend. I'll see if I can get you a phone number. I don't know if she has any left or not."

"That's okay. We'll call and find out," I said.

We didn't realize it then, but we had just begun a journey toward becoming much more than a one-dog family.

Cool, we thought. It's always fun to look at puppies. It can be dangerous, though. It's hard to look at that those cute little guys and not take one home.

Talking and thinking about looking at some new puppies put us in a really good mood and sent us on a buying frenzy at the ski fair. We hadn't really planned on getting much of anything. I needed poles, because I had broken one right at the end of last ski season. We ended up buying two sets of new snowshoes, two pair of used skating skis, boots for Betsy, some odds and ends, and, yes, a new set of poles for me. The total was well over $300. We had already purchased new down jackets and, of course, earlier that year we bought our first all-wheel-drive vehicle, a Subaru station wagon. We were ready for whatever the Lake Effect snow machine could throw at us. Let winter begin.

Then we waited all that winter for winter to begin. Never before had we been so ready, and never was winter quite so absent. What a disappointment. One good thing about the seasons, though: They come back again and again, so there's always next year.

We took the phone number from John and arranged to see the puppies. There was an inch or so of snow on the ground, just enough to tease us.

Now, Husky puppies, in my experience, are not universally cute. Many are, but some are kind of, well—funny looking. Their eyes appear to be too close together, their ears sometimes too big for their head, or their legs too long for their body. I don't remember the name of the girl who owned the pups or what she looked like. But I do remember those pups. They were cute. Cute, cute, cute. There was one that was nearly all white that my wife favored, and a black-and-white one that I favored.

"What do you think?" I asked Betsy.

"They are so-o-o cute," she responded.

Did I mention how cute they were?

She turned to the girl. "How much are you asking for them?"

"$150."

This was a good price for Husky pups, we thought.

"They aren't registered yet, but they can be," said the girl.

This was a detail that was not really important to either of us. Betsy and I looked at each other. She was still holding the white one, and I was still holding the black-and-white one.

"We'll think about it," Betsy said. She turned to me. "As cute as these guys are, I'm not sure I'm ready for a puppy. And it's not the best time of year to get a puppy." We prefer to get puppies in the spring. Housebreaking seems a bit easier for both dog and human. She continued, "And we just got Bayley through his—"

"I know," I interrupted.

"Besides, if we do get a dog, I want one that we can use this year."

"You're right."

Thus, as hard as it was to leave those puppies, we did. Betsy put down the white one, and I put down the black-and-white one.

Betsy turned to the girl. "We'll let you know. But if you have an opportunity to sell them, don't wait for us. They really are cute."

"Thanks," said the girl. "It's gonna be hard to see them go."

That was good to hear. Good breeders really care about their dogs. When we bought Leo, the breeder took a picture of us with our new puppy. She then proceeded to cry a little bit. She told us that she always cries when she sells a puppy.

We went home and told Bayley that we had decided not to get a puppy at this time. He seemed relieved. Although he missed Leo, he kind of liked the idea of being an only dog. After all, he had Tucker, our black Himalayan cat, to keep him company when we weren't home. And Tucker, though not enamored with dogs in general, liked to have at least one dog around the house that he could boss around. So there it was. One dog, one cat, two humans. At the time, it seemed like the way things ought to be. Bayley and Betsy would ski together, I would ski as I always had, and Tucker would stay at home and be our watch cat. I informed Bayley and Tucker of our plan. Bayley looked at me with some cynicism.

Tucker? he thought, *Our watch cat? I think I can handle the skiing part, but I don't know about Tuck.*

"He'll be great," I reassured Bayley. Then I turned to Tucker. "Whaddaya think, Tuck? Defender of the home, guardian of the Waterman household. You think you can handle it?" I got a little carried away.

Tucker looked at me with that typical cat look and gave me a big yawn. He then turned, leaped up on the couch, curled up, and went to sleep. Why did I even have to ask?

We got a couple of early snows, enough to ski on, but we didn't get a chance to do any skiing until after Christmas. Christmas is a fun time for us. Decorating alone takes considerable time. Betsy does a fantastic job of getting the house ready. Our home always has what one friend described as a 'friendly elegance,' but at this time of year, there's a kind of magic that's added. I love walking into our house at Christmas time. Our tree, which we get as early in the season as we can, is decorated with all white lights, old-style broad paper ribbons, and musical instrument ornaments. I believe we have an entire orchestra on our tree by now. We also put on some real candles, but we don't light them, except for that one New Year's Eve …

After Christmas, though, we're ready to strike the set. It's time to get on with winter things, like cross-country skiing, and, although snow was generally in meager supply that winter, occasionally we were blessed with just enough snow. Even a light snow year usually yields some skiing. It's true that we can have no snow in Sandy Creek, but drive ten miles to the east, to Tug Hill, and find snow. Such was the case this year.

We knew there was snow "up east," as we locals are wont to say. The area where we do most of our skiing is part of the Winona State Forest. One of the ways you can tell a non-local is how they refer to this part of Tug Hill. If they say something like, "We love skiing in Winona Forest," then you know they are not from the area. Everyone knows you ski "up on the Tug" or "up east." It sounds like some great distance to travel, a bit like the Wise Men, but for us it's a few short miles away.

We do share the area with snowmobilers. However, they are limited to the unplowed roads. That still leaves us with forty to fifty miles of trails for skiing and makes it a cooperative, rather than competitive, arrangement. Plus, there are hundreds of other groomed, interconnecting snowmobile trails on Tug Hill. Skiers stay off those trails, and the snowmobilers stay off the ski trails. It seems to be an acceptable situation for everyone.

We decided to try Bayley on harness with Betsy. It was a weekday, right after the start of the new year. I didn't have any massages scheduled, and Betsy was between semesters. Weekdays usually meant that there weren't a lot of people on the trails. We drove to Wart Road, the closest entrance point to the trails. As anticipated, there were only a few cars in the parking lot. We got ready and took off. The conditions were pretty good—not really fast, but not slow either. I was anxious to get going. Since this was Bayley's first time at this, it was taking a couple of extra minutes.

"Hike! Hike!" Betsy shouted.

We thought we knew the proper commands. We had read the book. We had the words, the proper equipment. We thought we were pretty hot stuff. Of course, we still didn't know if we had the proper dog, but that's what we were trying to find out.

Bayley did well at first. As it had been with Betsy and Leo, Betsy and Bayley soon disappeared over the first little hill. I snuck over the crest of the hill just in time to see them turn right onto Winona Way. As I turned, too, I could see them ahead of me.

"All right," I thought. "Bay and Bets are doing great."

I was gradually closing the gap on them. Winona Way is basically uphill on this portion, with only a couple little down-hills. This gave me a slight advantage. Bayley was certainly not in any shape to pull Betsy up the hills with any speed, and Betsy, though she keeps herself in fairly good shape, doesn't work out to near the intensity that I do. This has always been part of the problem. Actually, the bulk of the problem.

"I want it to be fun, not work," is her favorite line.

I understand, but for me, work is part of the fun. "The better shape you're in, the more you can enjoy the sport," is my favorite comeback. Still, I had decided that I would stay with her, dog or not. I really wasn't trying to martyr myself, either. I just wanted to stay with her. However, with Bayley doing as well as he was, it was like old times. Betsy and I could stay together with the help of "the world's best dog."

We finished our ski, cutting across Sally's Ride, down Hawley Road, and back out Wart Road to the car. We made a couple of brief rest stops along the way. The distance is about four and a half miles, a good start for the first time out. Bayley had done great. We were very encouraged. This might work after all.

Later in the week, we went out again. This time didn't go so well. Bayley, who seemed to have such a good time before, just did not have his heart in it. We took a slightly different route. Our plan was to go out Wart Road to Hawley, turn left onto Hawley, ski to where Winona Way intersects with Hawley, and turn left onto Winona Way. Ski to Hiscock, go left on Hiscock to Wart Road, left onto Wart Road and back to the car. This would be a little farther than we had gone the first time. However, when we got to Winona Way, it was obvious that Bayley was struggling.

"Something's wrong with Bayley," Betsy said as she approached the turn onto Winona Way. "He's not doing well at all. I think his leg is bothering him."

"I see that," I responded. "He doesn't look good." Actually, he looked horrible. His tail was dragging, his head and ears were down, and he really wasn't pulling. This dog was not having a good time.

"I think I'm going to let him off and let him run alongside us for a while."

Betsy took off his harness and let him go. Instant personality change. Bayley's ears perked up, and he began acting like a puppy. "Oh goody, I'm free," is what he appeared to be thinking.

"Well, he doesn't seem to be hurting now, does he?" I commented.

"Nope. I don't know what his problem is," Betsy said in confusion. "He did so well the other day. He seemed to enjoy it before. I just don't understand."

"What do you want to do now?"

"I don't like Bayley running free."

"Yeah, but there really isn't anybody around today."

"I'd like to finish our ski," said Betsy. "How far are we from Hiscock?"

Hiscock is a nice little trail. The direction we were going made it primarily downhill, with a few dips and doodles to make it more interesting.

"Not far," I answered. "We shouldn't have any trouble getting out before dark." We had started midafternoon, but this time of year, night comes early.

We started up Winona Way and skied together to where Hiscock intersects. We stayed together for a short time, but Betsy knew I wanted to go faster.

"Why don't you go on ahead?"

"Are you sure?" I asked.

"Yeah. I'll be right behind you."

A free-running Bayley and I took off together. Though there are no big hills on Hiscock, with a little effort, you can build up pretty good speed. When I got to Wart Road, I stopped to wait for Betsy. After a few minutes I decided to go back and meet her. We met up after I'd gone back a couple of hundred yards. She was crying.

"What's the matter?" I asked.

"I miss Leo," she answered.

In among the sobs, she continued, "It's gonna be just like it was before (sob). You're either gonna be way ahead of me (sob) and we'll each be skiing alone (sob) or you'll hold back, ski with me, feel martyred (sob), and I'll feel like the bad witch of the north 'cause I'm making you ski with me (sob)."

I tried to reassure her. "No, hon. I really don't mind skiing with you."

She wasn't convinced. She continued to cry. I gave her a hug. Not an easy thing to do when both parties are on skis and holding on to poles. Bayley leaped up on Betsy also trying to reassure her. He stretched up as far as he could so he could give her a kiss. Bayley always tries to cheer us up.

"It's okay, Bayley. It's not your fault, is it, boy?" Betsy said.

We continued on, staying together, but Betsy was not happy. The "Bayley helping her out" plan seemed doomed at this point. We got back to the parking lot and put our skis on the rack. The three of us climbed in the car and started home.

Betsy was quiet. She was thinking. Finally, she looked up and quite suddenly said, "We're going to have to get another dog."

"Yep." Sometimes I amaze myself with the intelligent responses I give.

"Why don't we get a Sunday paper and see if there are any dogs for sale."

"That's a good idea."

The hunt for another dog, preferably a Siberian Husky, was on.

That Sunday, we stopped at the local Big M Market and bought a paper. We were on our way to Watertown to do some shopping. I drove so Betsy could mull over the classifieds to see what she could find. It took a few minutes to find the classifieds. Sunday papers have so much extra stuff. Anyway, Betsy found the classified section and sorted her way through to "Pets." There it was: just what we were looking for:

Siberian Husky. Purebred with papers. One year old.
Female.
Silver colored, with brown eyes. $190. Call 699-xxxx.

Betsy read the ad to me, then said, "I'm going to call her."

"Right now?" I asked.

"Why not? What's the sense in waiting?"

"I guess you might as well," I answered.

Betsy picked up the cell phone and made the call.

"Hi. I'm calling about the Husky you have for sale. My first question is: Why are you selling her? ... I see ... Uh-huh ... When can we come see her? How about tomorrow morning? ... Great. Thanks a lot ... Oh, I need directions on how to get to your house." Betsy proceeded to take down a set of very detailed instructions. She read them back to the woman to make sure she had it all down right. Then I heard her ask, "Is there a sign out front? ... Oh, okay. Thanks a lot. We'll see you then."

"What'd she have to say?" I asked

"The dog sounds like a really good dog."

"Then why are they selling her?"

"She raises Huskies for show. What she does is take the two best puppies from each litter and sends them to a trainer. Then, when they're a year old, she keeps the one that has shown the best in puppy shows and sells the other one. That's the one that's in the paper. I'd like to go see her tomorrow. Can you go with me?"

"Yes," I answered. "Where is she, anyway?"

"Somewhere near Cicero."

"That's not very far," I said.

"I told her we'd try to get there around ten."

We finished our shopping and went home. The next morning, we headed down to Cicero. We were both excited. This is just what we wanted—a young dog, one that's been trained, housebroken, and has had all its shots. We would just have to spay her. We were a little concerned that she had been trained to show. We didn't want a dog for show. We wanted a dog that would pull. Still, we kept telling ourselves that

Huskies have pulling in their blood. We were sure it would work out.

It was a good thing she gave us detailed directions to her home. This was in our pre-GPS days. It was in a housing development with cul-de-sacs everywhere. We wound our way through and miraculously found her house. We parked our car, walked up to the front door, and rang the doorbell. She greeted us and invited us in.

"C'mon in," she said as she motioned with her hand. "I'm Linda. Don't mind the mess. I run a small daycare, too."

I looked around. There were small children seemingly everywhere.

"Two of them are mine, and I take care of four others. It makes for a busy day, but I enjoy it."

The house was a split-level. When you enter the house, there's a half flight of stairs going up to the main floor and a half flight of stairs going down to the basement area. She led us down to the basement where the dogs were. There were about ten or so crates lined up along the wall, all occupied by gorgeous Huskies. One of them had pups. They were all silver colored.

"These are my dogs," she said with pride. "I breed them for show, but also for temperament. In fact, temperament comes first."

"They're all beautiful, and the puppies are adorable," said Betsy.

"They sure are," I chirped in.

"Where is the one you're selling?" Betsy asked.

"She's outside. She just started blowing her coat."

Huskies have an outer coat and an inner coat. This is what makes them so adapted for cold weather. It's the inner coat that they shed, or "blow," twice a year. Most of the time,

Huskies shed very little. However, when they blow their coats, it is impressive. One can literally grab huge handfuls of fur off their bodies. A normally beautiful dog becomes scraggly looking. That was the case this time. She led us outside. We both noted that she looked very skinny, also.

"Come 'ere Spearmint, come 'ere, girl," she called.

"What's her name?" I asked, not quite sure I had heard correctly.

"Well, her real name is Spirit, but I don't like it," she responded. "So I decided to call her Spearmint."

"Oh," we both said. We looked at each other, and Betsy whispered, "I don't know why she would do that. I like the name Spirit."

I nodded in agreement. We approached Spirit. She slunk back behind Linda with her ears down. So far Spirit was not making much of an impression.

We called to her, "Come 'ere Spirit, come 'ere Spirit." Reluctantly, she came over to us, then backed off before we could touch her.

"I don't know what's wrong with her. Up until a couple of days ago, she was friendly and happy. I think what happened is there were some men doing work in the house, and they left the front door open. Spirit started toward the door and I lunged at her and grabbed her. Ever since then she's acted funny."

I realize now that sometimes you have to make Herculean efforts to not let a Husky escape. They may take off and run and run. They may run so far they can't find their way back.

"Do you know if she's ever pulled anything?" asked Betsy.

"I think Beth, the trainer, told me that Spirit pulled her husband on his bicycle once or twice, but that's about all."

"We want to use her for skijoring," Betsy said.

Spirit

We then chatted with her for a while about how we wanted to use Spirit to pull Betsy on her skis; told her about the sport; told her about Leo and Bayley and how Bayley couldn't pull her because of his past injuries.

"She's underweight now. The trainer thinks that Huskies should be thin. I don't think she fed her enough."

Betsy and I agreed that she was too thin. She also continued to act very skittish around us. We still weren't convinced this was the dog for us.

"I don't know," Betsy said as her voice trailed off.

"Let me get her sister and a couple of the other dogs. Maybe she'll perk up."

While Linda went to get the other dogs, Betsy and I expressed our reservations.

"I still am not convinced. I'm concerned about her shyness." Betsy said.

"Me, too." I have been told, affectionately I'm sure, that I am a man of few words.

Just then, Linda reappeared with three more Huskies. She called one of them over. She identified one of them as Spirit's sister. She looked a lot like Spirit, except that she wasn't blowing her coat and she had that bounding Husky personality.

"This is what Spirit is normally like," she said.

We were still skeptical. Spirit had not perked up much with the addition of the other dogs. Linda then made one last plea.

"How about you take her for a few days? Somebody called and wants to use her as a watchdog in a big orchard. I'm afraid that she wouldn't get very good care. If you have her, I can at least tell them that the dog is gone. You don't have to pay me or anything unless you decide to keep her."

After meeting Spirit's sister, we could certainly see the potential. And we hated to think that this shy, frightened dog would be chained in someone's orchard day after day, pretending to be a guard dog. We agreed and took Spirit home with us. After all, we had nothing to lose.

❄ ❄ ❄

Spirit hopped into the car with no reservations. She was used to being transported because of her show training. On the way home, she crawled to the front of the car and gave me a great big, ole slobbery kiss. In return, I scratched her ears and head, then told her to get in the back. As she did, she quickly turned and gave Betsy, who was driving, a quick lick. She was starting to work her way into our hearts, and we weren't even home yet. We arrived home and introduced her to Bayley. That went very smoothly. After a few initial sniffs, they accepted each other readily. We put them out in the fence together and watched them interact. Spirit relieved herself almost immediately, then played with Bayley in a reserved sort of way.

After a while, both dogs appeared at the back door. They both sat there patiently waiting for us to open the door and let them in. This was a big plus. Leo, as nice a dog as he was, would paw at the door, leaving it dirty and scratched. It drove Betsy crazy. Fortunately, Bayley had not learned this bad habit from Leo. And now it appeared that we had another dog who didn't paw and scratch. It was quite charming to look out the French doors and see two dogs sitting, looking hopeful that a human would come to let them in.

"Please, Mom and Dad, let us in. It's cold out here," they were saying. We thought it was kind of early for Spirit to call us Mom and Dad. I guess she had already made up her mind to stay.

We let them in the house. Bayley came over to me, and Spirit went over to Betsy. Spirit immediately began to wash Betsy's face. There was a gentleness about it. I could tell that Betsy was hooked. Spirit had found her home. I was happy about it, too. In spite of our reservations about her, we knew that Spirit was a pretty special dog. We decided to wait for a few days before calling Linda and telling her that we were keeping Spirit, but we had pretty much made up our minds.

A couple of days later, Betsy called Linda.

"Hi Linda. This is Betsy Waterman."

"Oh hi," came the response. "How's Spearmint doing?"

"She's doing pretty well. We've decided to keep her. After all, we wouldn't want her banished to some orchard."

"Great."

"She still acts a little shy, but other than that, she's a sweetie. And she gets along with Bayley and our cat."

"I knew you'd want her once you got to know her a little bit."

We were now the proud owners of a show-quality Siberian Husky. But will she pull? We would soon find out.

Chapter 5

A Two-Dog Family

Spirit fit into our household very well. She was extremely well-behaved. She didn't jump on people, she didn't bang against the door when she wanted to come in, she was quiet, and she was very loving. She was everything most people would want in a pet. Unfortunately, we wanted just one thing more. We wanted a dog to pull Betsy on her skis. When we first got Spirit, there wasn't enough snow to ski on. As you may recall, I said this was a very light winter. In fact, it warmed up enough that our first trial with her came on inline skates. We had already purchased a harness for her. We were quite optimistic. After all, she was a Siberian Husky, a proud descendent of the dogs who helped the Chukchi people survive the harsh winters of Siberia. Alas, no one had told Spirit that.

We took Bayley and Spirit over to the fairgrounds. We hooked up the dogs, side by side. I held them until Betsy gave the command.

"Let's go!" Betsy called out in her best musher voice. After being so proud that we knew we were supposed to say "hike" to tell our dogs to start running, we had since learned that most mushers didn't actually use the term "hike," and simply used the phrase "let's go," which made sense to us.

Bayley took off like a dog on a mission. He didn't mind pulling a person on inline skates. It's much easier than pulling a person on skis. Spirit, on the other hand, merely looked confused.

"What's this?" she seemed to say. "I was bred to be beautiful, and I do that very well. I was not bred to do manual labor like some commoner."

As a result, Bayley ended up not only pulling Betsy around the parking lot, but Spirit as well. We were quite discouraged. I even took Spirit over to the fairgrounds myself. Sometimes, if you work a dog one on one, you get better results. We got to the fairgrounds. Spirit reluctantly got out of the car. I tried to maintain a positive attitude.

"Here we are, Spirit. C'mon girl. We're gonna go roller blading," I said in my cheeriest voice.

Spirit was not impressed. I got us hooked up, gave the command, and off we went, Spirit running reluctantly next to me, head down. No amount of encouragement helped. The only thing Spirit did with any enthusiasm was hop in the car when we were done. We now were the proud owners of two dogs that wouldn't, or couldn't, pull Betsy on her skis. Bayley didn't have the physical stamina, and Spirit just didn't have the interest.

This left us in quite a quandary. We simply wouldn't give Bayley away. He is, after all, the world's best dog. And Spirit had quickly worked her way into our hearts, especially Betsy's. Don't get me wrong. I really liked Spirit, too. It's just that a special bond had developed between Spirit and Betsy. And between Spirit and Bayley. In truth, just about everyone who met Spirit liked her. What's not to like? She's beautiful, friendly, quiet, intelligent—all the things you'd want in a dog, unless you wanted a guard dog or one that would pull you on skis.

There was one thing that bothered us. Sometimes she was too quiet. In fact, she often acted like a twelve-year-old dog rather than a one-year-old. We had done enough research to know that Huskies are supposed to be lively, energetic, bouncy, and glad to be alive. This was not Spirit. There were days when she didn't seem to want to get out of bed. When she did finally get herself moving, she walked around with her head down and her ears back. There was no Husky smile. Betsy and I knew that something was wrong.

"She acts like an old dog," Betsy explained to the vet.

"Well, let's take a look," replied the vet.

He gave her a good once-over and explained, "I can't find anything obviously wrong with her. Her heart seems strong, and I don't find any problems in the gut area."

"That may be, but there has to some reason why she acts like she does," I said.

"What I could do is some blood work. I'll send samples to Cornell and see if they come up with anything. It's kind of expensive, though."

Cornell University in Ithaca, New York, has a large veterinary school and animal research facility.

"That's okay," Betsy and I both answered together. What's money, anyway?

Then the vet continued, "You know, there are a lot of people who would love a dog like this."

"That may be," answered Betsy, "but something is wrong. She just doesn't act like a young dog. "

"We'll see what Cornell has to say."

"Okay. When will you know something?"

"Oh, probably a week to ten days," came the answer.

Have you ever noticed that everything seems to take a week to ten days? What that really means is: We haven't a clue, but if we're lucky, we might have an answer by the time you call back. Oh yeah—and if we tell you we'll call you when the results are back, we really may not.

Ten days later, we called back.

"As I suspected, the blood work didn't really show anything," said the vet. "There were a few highs and lows, but nothing out of the ordinary, and nothing to cause the symptoms that you describe."

"Thanks," said Betsy as she hung up the phone. Then she turned to me and said, "They didn't really find anything. He said that there were some 'highs and lows,' but nothing to worry about. I guess it's back to square one."

"What did he mean by a few highs and lows?" I asked.

"He didn't really explain, except to say that everything is still within normal limits."

There is nothing more frustrating than a good non-answer.

❄ ❄ ❄

We were now approaching spring. Occasionally, we tried Spirit with our inline skates, and occasionally she showed signs of pulling. In general, though, she just ran alongside. We were becoming a little frustrated. It wouldn't have been so hard if she weren't such a good dog in every other way. Still, we wanted our dogs to be working dogs as well as pets. I suggested we call the mushers Art and Karen to see if they had ever dealt with a dog that wouldn't pull. Betsy made the call.

"Oh, sure," answered Karen when asked if they ever had a dog that didn't seem to want to pull.

"What do you do with them?" asked Betsy.

"Well, Art doesn't have any patience with them, and so he just doesn't do anything with them if they don't naturally pull. But I work with them, and now some of our best dogs are dogs that at first wouldn't pull. I think it's just that sometimes they aren't sure what they're supposed to do. Once they get the hang of it, off they go."

"How do they get the hang of it?" Betsy asked.

"You have to try different things. Sometimes I put them with a small team so there's less pressure on them, and sometimes I work with them alone. You have to experiment to see what's going to work. Don't give up on her yet, though. How old is she?"

"A year."

"Oh, she's young yet. She'll come around. Just be patient with her, and don't push too hard."

"Thanks, Karen."

"No problem. If you need any help, just call. We got lots of help from other people when we started out. We'd be glad to do whatever we can."

That's the nice thing about being associated with mushers. In general, everyone cooperates and helps each other out as much as possible. We had always been impressed by the cooperation among mushers. This seemed particularly apparent at races, where there are hyper dogs all over the place. Though everyone is obviously responsible for his or her own dogs, everyone also helps out when getting ready for a race, helping hold a team as they are getting ready to run.

Karen's conversation was somewhat reassuring but still a little frustrating. It was long on encouragement, but short on detail. We knew to be patient, but what techniques, exactly, did she use? We didn't have a team to run her with, only Bayley, and he was somewhat fickle. I must admit also that at times Spirit did pull. Betsy took her out once, and Spirit actually pulled her for a short distance. She did this just often enough to encourage us *and* frustrate us. Why one time and not another left us completely baffled. Now we had two dogs that were totally unpredictable in terms of pulling.

That spring, I got back into my running routine. I do most of my running on the fairgrounds' track. It's a half mile long and dirt, making it a relatively good surface to run on. It's also pretty much enclosed, which means I can let the dogs run free with me. For the first couple of laps, the dogs just run and run. After that, they settle down and stay with me. It's a good time for us all.

The only time this is a problem is when the Oswego County Fair is being held. Lately, the fair has been held at the end of June through the beginning of July, ending around the Fourth of July with a big fireworks display. The fair is a combination of traditional types of events and things you won't even find on ESPN2. There are, of course, the pie judging, the photography judging, the baby judging, the cattle-horse-pig-chicken-duck-rabbit-and-other-assorted-rodent judging. If you do well here, you go to the New York State Fair at the end of the summer to compete with other county fair winners.

Then there are the grandstand events. These are things that you seem to find only at county fairs. There is the ever-popular demolition derby, in which drivers run their cars into each other until only one car is left running. The ideal car for this is an old clunker with a massive front end, since it's the radiator that is most vulnerable. Another popular event is car football. In this event, there are three cars on a team. The object is to push a huge, round ball (not shaped like an American football at all) across a line. Again, old cars are used.

It's really another demolition derby with a ball thrown into the middle. It is amazing what entertains us.

Then, of course, we have the tractor pulls. When I was a kid, a tractor pull consisted of some local farmers bringing their tractors to the fair and seeing who could pull the most weight. A sled loaded with cement blocks was used. In to-day's tractor pulls, the basic idea is the same. The difference is in the tractors. These are not machines you would ever see in a farm field. They more closely resemble dragsters than tractors. And the people running them are not farmers, but professionals who go from event to event.

The worst part of tractor pulls is the noise. It's not a con-stant noise, but approximately ten seconds of R-R-R-O-A-R, followed by just enough relative quiet to doze off to sleep if you happen to live close by. We do, in fact, live close by. All of the grandstand events sound like they are taking place in our backyard. Fortunately, they aren't. After a while, we lay there, trying not to fall asleep for fear of being rudely awakened. We ask each other:

"Do you suppose that was the last one?"

"It has been a while," one of us answers.

We lay back, convinced the pulling is over, and allow our-selves to go to sleep. Then, R-R-R-O-A-R! We sit bolt upright in bed, and the whole scenario repeats itself. Still, all in all, we look forward to the fair. There is always lots of good food.

And sometimes you even get a line on a dog. Such was the case the summer after we got Spirit. While strolling through the history building, we ran into some friends of ours. They have a son who shows cattle, so they set up a little camper trailer and spend most of the time right on the fairgrounds. As a result, they get to know most everybody at the fair. They also raise Border Collies, so our conversation quickly turned to dogs. We explained our situation to them. They knew Bayley's story, but didn't know about Spirit. We told them that if we ever got another Husky, we would get one out of sled dog stock.

As luck would have it, and as is typically the case in such conversations, Mary said, "We know just the person. He's manning the two-cylinder tractor club booth. We were chatting with him just a little while ago and found out that he also has Siberian Husky puppies for sale. He used to race his dogs, so I expect they are out of sled dog stock."

"Over at the two-cylinder booth?" I repeated.

"Yeah."

"Great. We'll go over and talk with him."

I realize that some of you may not know what the two-cylinder tractor club means. Antique John Deere tractors, up until the mid-1950s, had only two cylinders. It gave the tractor quite a distinct sound.

We headed over to the booth. As we approached, we saw a tall, thin man sitting at a table in front of eight or nine freshly painted, antique John Deere tractors. He looked up at us from beneath his brand-new John Deere hat and asked, "Can I help you folks?"

"Yeah. Are you the fellow who raises sled dogs?" I asked. "Some friends of ours said somebody over here does."

"Yep, that's right," he answered. "Got some puppies for sale right now. I got one that's nine weeks old. Nice lookin' little girl. She could go right now. And I got some others that are younger. I got one litter of pups about five weeks and another about two weeks old. Some of them are already sold, but I still have several left."

"And these all come from sled dog stock?" Betsy inquired.

"Yep."

"And they're all purebred Siberians?"

"Yep. I got papers for every one of them."

"Great," Betsy said. "We bought a dog from show stock. She's a wonderful dog, but she just doesn't seem to want to pull."

"These dogs'll run. Haven't had one yet that didn't."

"That's what we need. When can we take a look at them?"

"Well, let me see, now. I gotta finish up here." He paused for a moment. "I'll be mostly home next week. Call me then and we'll set somethin' up. Here's my card."

He picked up a business card. It read:

Robert Irons
Two-Cylinder Tractor Club
Siberian Husky Sled Dogs

Then it listed his address and phone number.

My favorite business card, though, was for a professional tuba player who had retired and then later joined a village police force. Under his name it said: *Tuba and Pistol Instruction.* How handy, I thought when I first saw his card. Now, when a mugger comes from behind you and grabs your tuba, you can defend yourself.

Betsy pointed to the address on the card. "Where is this?" she asked.

"Up near Carthage."

Carthage is small village about fifty minutes to an hour away.

"Okay," Betsy said. "We'll give you a call sometime next week."

We all said our "nice meeting yous" and continued our stroll around the fair.

"Boy, the one that's nine weeks sounds tempting," Betsy said. "I think we should at least take a look at her. By winter she will be big enough to do a little pulling."

"I agree," I said.

So it was. We continued to meander around the fairgrounds for a while, but most of our conversation centered around the possibility that we were soon to become a three-dog family: two dogs that really didn't work as skijor dogs, but ones that we loved with all our hearts—and one that would potentially be Betsy's skijor partner. It was getting dark, so we headed back to our house.

❄ ❄ ❄

The next week, Betsy called to set up a time and got directions to Bob's house. It was one of those "you can't get there from here" kind of places: go north of Watertown, take a right onto route something-or-other, go east 'til you get to so-and-so's convenience store, go past the fire hall about two miles and look for the (what else?) John Deere mailbox on the left-hand side of the road.

"Either my wife or I should be up to the house," said Mr. Irons after he gave the directions. "If not, we'll be around somewhere."

"Okay," I responded.

I often take the phone when directions are given. Betsy is a very intelligent person, except when it comes to spatial things, which are generally my forte, although I have been known to screw up occasionally. My wife and I enjoy wilderness canoe camping. On one camping trip in Algonquin Park, Ontario, Canada, we left our campsite bright and early to get ahead of the afternoon winds that invariably come. I studied

the map and determined that we had to go around some is-
lands, through a channel, and turn right. I thought that's what
we had done. Still, it didn't look right. After three hours of
paddling and head-scratching, we finally discovered that we
had paddled back to our original campsite. But in the process,
we'd seen an awe-inspiring osprey fishing.

There would be no canoe involved this time, though. We
were excitedly headed north to check on a puppy that might
just become a part of our growing dog family. Bayley and Spirit
decided they wanted to come along, and they had popped up
on the back seat. It was a gorgeous summer day. The sun was
shining, and the temperature hovered in the upper seventies;
it was a little breezy with low humidity. The directions, which
had seemed a bit complex, took us right to Bob's home, a
small farm. We'd started toward the house when two women
appeared from a garden area at the back of the house.

"Hi," came a call from one of the women as they approached us. "Come on back. You must be the Watermans."

"That's right," Betsy answered.

"I'm Carol, Bob's wife. And this is Jen, a friend of mine."

"How do you do?" Jen greeted us.

"Fine, thanks," said Betsy. Then she turned toward Carol.
"I called about your dogs."

"Yes," Carol said. "Bob told me you would be coming. He's
out with the dogs right now. Follow me and I'll take you out
there."

We followed Carol down a narrow stone path, through
more gardens, to a series of dog pens. There was one small
barn surrounded by several dog pens with an exercise yard in
the middle. There were also two small whelping pens, both of
which were occupied. Though the pup in which we were most
interested, the nine-week-old, was not in either of these pens,

Muddy Neeka

the path took us right by them. Bob had heard us coming and was approaching from the back of the pens.

"Those there are two-week-olds," he said in a low, slow voice, gesturing toward one of the pens. It contained a very nervous-looking mother dog with about six puppies. The mom was nearly all white, but her pups were of various coloration.

"That mom is pretty protective, so you have to be a little careful around her. When she doesn't have pups, she's as friendly as can be, but when she's got babies, she can be a little snippy."

"Oh. That's okay," I said. "We understand."

He continued, "She'll let me git' in there with 'em, but I don't think she likes it much. Let me see if I can get one or two out for you."

Though the mom was uncomfortable, she allowed Bob to reach in and get a couple of pups. He handed one to each to us.

"We like to socialize our pups early. I think it makes a better dog."

"So do we," said Betsy as she carefully took one of the pups.

"In fact, our grandchildren come over after school and play with the pups. We pay them to socialize the puppies. They do a great job with them. They're very gentle."

"What a great idea," said Betsy.

"Yep. It's good for everybody. The grandkids get a little extra spending money, the pups get socialized, and we get to see our grandkids a lot."

We played with the small pups for a moment, then asked, "Where's the one that's nine weeks old?"

"Oh, she's out back here," he responded. "Her mom and dad are back here, too."

We handed the puppies back to Bob, who returned them to their relieved mom, and started back, when all of a sudden—CRASH! I about leaped out of my boots right then and there.

Without losing a beat, Bob said, "That's Rusty, the nine-week-old's dad. He gets a little excited when somebody comes back here."

A little excited? I would hate to see him *a lot* excited. He wasn't trying to go through or over the fence, but when he leaped, he was just a little out of control. This is typical Husky behavior. I will say this, though: Rusty was a beautiful dog, red and white. Although he was blowing his coat, he was still beautiful.

"And that one over there is the mom." He pointed to a long-haired black-and-white dog. She was built completely the opposite of her mate, Rusty. She was short-legged while he was very tall, and she was extremely long-haired while he was quite shorthaired. They certainly looked an odd couple.

"I just got her from Canada. Great championship lines. She only had two pups, a girl and a boy. I sold the boy. His sister back here is the one that I'm selling."

He took us to her pen. We looked at her, played with her for a minute, and made an offer, sort of.

"We'd like to think about it for a day or two. Is that all right?"

"Sure. Take all the time you need. Can you find your way back?" Bob asked. "I got just a little more work to do."

"No problem," we responded.

We headed back toward the car, stopping for a moment to say hello to Rusty and scratch his ears.

As we approached the car, we heard, "Are these your other dogs?" Carol had gone over to our car to visit Bayley and Spirit.

"Yeah. That's Bayley and Spirit," I responded.

"Boy, that silver one is a beautiful dog. We don't have any her color. I wouldn't mind trading one of our dogs for her."

"We aren't interested in trading her," Betsy said, slightly miffed at the thought. "And, besides, she is spayed."

"Oh," Carol said dejectedly.

A spayed dog is clearly of little value to a breeder.

We chatted for a few more minutes, and then left. On the way home, we discussed the pros and cons of getting another dog. The biggest holdup was whether or not we wanted to add another dog, period! On the one hand, taking care of three dogs seemed like a formidable task. On the other hand, if we don't get another dog, we might just as well forget about ski-joring for a while. Skijoring won out. We decided to buy the pup. Betsy called later that evening and told the Ironses our decision. They were quite pleased.

The next day, we headed back. We were filled with excitement, buffered by a little apprehension. As we approached the house, Bob came out to meet us.

"Come on in," he said and gestured. "We'll get all the paperwork done first."

"Have a seat," Carol said. "Buying a puppy is nearly as complex as buying a car."

"Here's her puppy book with her vet records, her registration forms. Now, you're going to have to send those in yourself. The address is on there somewhere. And here is her lineage chart. You can see that she comes from good racing stock. She's nine weeks old, so she'll be due for her twelve-week shots soon."

"Did you bring a leash?" asked Bill.

Oh man! How could we have forgotten a leash?

"That's okay. I'm sure I can find a piece o' rope or some-thin.'"

"Thanks."

We all walked out to the pen to retrieve the puppy that would become Neeka. She was a bright, lively pup, happy to see us. She knew how to get to me. She came over to me as I knelt over. She kind of sat, leaned into me, pushed her head into my chest, and reached up and gave me a little kiss. Bob took the rope and tied it around her neck. I grabbed the rope and started toward the car.

As we got to the car, Betsy picked up the pup and just before she got in the car, she asked Bob one more time, more as a challenge than a real question, "Do you promise me that she'll pull me on my skis?"

Bob looked at the pup, then at Betsy, and as he gave a nod with his John Deere hat and in a deep, Northern New York, don't-waste-words style, stated simply, "She'll run."

Chapter 6

What's in a Name?

Naming pets has always been a problem in our household. It took us two weeks to come up with Neeka's name. I know that some of you are thinking—it took you two weeks, and the best they could do is Neeka? What kind of a name is Neeka, anyway?

That's what our son Jeremy wondered, anyway. "Why can't you name her something more normal?"

The thing is, we almost always have a goal in naming pets. We shun the traditional royal names, like Lady, Princess, Duchess, or Queenie. Traditional names seem so, well, traditional. We've always had this problem, it seems. We also tend to stay away from people names, like Joe, Jed, or Charlie. I say this, and then I realize that most of our dogs have had a human name.

Our first dog, though, was named Muffin. I don't know why we named her Muffin; we just did. She was a mixed breed in every sense of the word, weighing in at about twenty-five pounds. She was the first puller we really had. Muffin enjoyed pulling almost as much as Leo did. We discovered this after our daughter Shelley was born in mid-November 1967. That winter we acquired a sled-type stroller. It was too hard for Betsy to manage the sled and the dog by herself. So one day she tied Muffin's leash to the sled. Muffin took off like a sled dog. From that time on, she went crazy every time we got out her leash or the sled (or, later, the regular stroller). Muffin also had one unusual quirk. She loved ice cubes. She loved them so much that she would take them and bury them in her little bed. The poor little thing was so confused when she went looking for them later and they had disappeared.

Our second dog, also for reasons that escape me, we named Oliver. He was a Bearded Collie mix who looked mostly like a Collie. My sister-in-law spent most of one summer with us and decided to do some obedience training with Oliver. It was certainly okay with us, and Oliver became a wonderfully behaved dog, but he also had a couple of odd quirks. He didn't like people wearing hats, and he hated cigarettes. One time on a walk, Oliver broke free from us. The next thing we knew, he was circling a man who was smoking a cigarette. The man was obviously frightened.

We yelled out, "Drop the cigarette. He doesn't like the cigarette."

The man looked at us, now confused and frightened.

"PUT OUT THE CIGARETTE! THE CIGARETTE!" I yelled.

This time the man got the idea. In one motion, he threw the cigarette on the ground and snuffed it with his foot. Immediately, Oliver became his normally friendly self. The man went on his merry, smoke-free way, a bit shaken, but none the worse for wear. Around our house, the phrase "No smoking if you value your life" took on an immediacy as long as Oliver was around, which unfortunately was not very long.

Oliver died young, at only five. He had cried a bit in the night. We reached over the bed to his spot on the floor and gently patted him. He seemed uneasy, and soon was asking to go outside. *Perhaps he has a bit of an upset stomach,* we thought, *and simply needs to go to the bathroom.* We opened the door, and he quietly moved outside. When we called him to come in, he resisted, and seemed content to lie on the front porch. We returned to bed and awoke early to check on him. When we opened the door, what we saw shocked us.

Oliver was bloated and clearly in terrible pain. We contacted the on-call vet and carried him to the car. The vet met us at the back door of the clinic. As we carried him into the office, Oliver died. The vet explained that Oliver had suffered from gastric torsion; his stomach had turned over and his intestines had become blocked. By the time it's diagnosed, it's often too late. Oliver was a gentle, intelligent dog. It hurt deeply to lose him.

Our next dog was Thor. He was named after the god of thunder in Greek mythology. At 110 pounds, he was big, all black, and very intimidating looking. In actuality, he was nothing but a big puffball. Thor was a magnificent beast. He was a stray that had shown up at Betsy's dad's house one day. He appeared to be a Newfoundland (and, perhaps, Irish Setter) mix. He was very quiet. There were only two things that could excite him: birds and helicopters. Since we live along Interstate 81, a supply route for Fort Drum, we see military helicopters quite often. It didn't take long for the pilots to learn that if they flew over the Waterman homestead, a big black dog would give them a merry chase down or up our long driveway, and so they came back again and again.

Thor was a gentle dog. At some point, we acquired a stray white cat. We named her Panger. I have no recollection of how we chose that name. It didn't take long after she showed up on our doorstep to realize that she was pregnant. She was not a particularly good mother. Her seven mostly white,

109

black-capped babies would wander away from the nest, and she would just let them go. Soon they discovered Thor. He would lie there and let those little white fur balls climb all over him. It wasn't long before he took over a surrogate parent role. Panger, trying to be ever so helpful, seized this opportunity, and would *bring* the kittens to Thor. Then, while he was watching them, she took a nap. It got to the point where the only time she saw her babies was when she fed them, but Thor never complained.

Thor had become great friends with our elderly neighbor and would go to visit her once a day. She would give him treats, and he would sit with her for hours. One day Betsy got a call. It was the neighbor, who was crying and said that Thor was lying under the big tree in her front yard and that he could not get up. It was raining hard. Betsy climbed into the car and rushed to our neighbor's house.

Thor raised his head, and his tail thumped when he saw Betsy. Betsy had called the vet, but the challenge now was to get 110 pounds of dead weight into the backseat of the car. Somehow, she managed it, with a little help from our neighbor. Thor had been a bit lame on and off for weeks, but the vet had said it was arthritis, and that there was little that could be done. Betsy knew it was time for Thor to be released from this life. She called me at work and, while I couldn't get away, I told her that I agreed, and Thor peacefully left this life.

We were never sure of his age, but we guessed he was about twelve or thirteen years old when he died. A good, long life for such a big dog. I do know that after he died, we saw less and less of the helicopters directly overhead.

After Thor came Leo. I realize that is also a people name, but as you recall, he was named after a historical figure. That somehow makes it okay.

When we added Neeka to our home, we wanted a Chukchi or Siberian name that meant "wolf." Even though Huskies are no more wolf than any dog, we thought it would be cool. We searched the Internet, with no results. We made up a couple of names that sounded Russian, at least to us. I believe they were something like Miska, Meeska, and other variations. Finally, I found a list of Russian names online. It turns out that Russians don't name their children Wolf—what a surprise.

I saw the name Neeka, which means, "blessed one." It's not exactly what we had been looking for, but I ran it by Betsy, and she agreed; it was time to name the dog and get on with life. We ran it by our children. They were less than enthusiastic about it, but they couldn't come with anything better either. So that's how our little red Husky pup became Neeka.

Neeka had a normal puppyhood. Peeing where she shouldn't pee, pooping where she shouldn't poop, chewing on what she shouldn't chew on, and digging where she shouldn't dig. And like all Huskies, she didn't stay where she should stay, unless she was fenced in or tied. Tying has just never worked for us; a fence has always been our primary way of keeping dogs in. As you may recall, however, we had lost Bayley out of a fence on several occasions, so we knew we needed something foolproof.

Earlier in the year, we believed we had solved the fence problem. A local lumberyard was selling out of "invisible fencing." We started out fairly small, enclosing about an acre at first. An acre to a lot of people would seem like plenty of room, but when you own forty acres, it seems pretty small. The radio fencer was good for 100 acres. I figured it was a shame to waste all that power, and why not give the dogs lots of room to run?

Perhaps I should regress and explain how invisible fencing works. It's simple, really. A controller inside your house or garage sends a continuous radio signal out through a wire, which is then buried about two inches below the surface of the ground. In our case, though, since most of the wire went through the woods, we just left it on the surface. The dogs wear a receiver collar. As the pet approaches the wire, a warning sound goes off. If the dogs continue, the collar gives them a little electrical shock. For many dogs, one experience with the shock is enough. So, anyway, we decided to give it a try.

After we laid enough to cover about an acre, we began to think bigger. I should say *I* began to think bigger. Betsy seemed quite content with the amount of wire we had already put down. I decided it would be great for the dogs if we enclosed an area that would include a portion of our stream. This meant re-rolling a portion of the wire, re-laying it, and splicing in additional wire. It also meant forging the stream. I found an old piece of half-inch hose to run the wire through and buried it as best I could in the streambed.

Next, I forced the wire through the hose—not an easy task, I might add. The wire would get about three-quarters of the way through and get hung up on something. After about half an hour of pushing, pulling back, and cursing, I was still not successful. I then decided that if I could find an easier way, I would take it. I ran the wire along the opposite shore until I came to a dead tree that had conveniently fallen across the stream. I was able to lay the wire on the tree, a much easier solution. From there, I followed our woods trail back to the house. We now had about five acres enclosed.

"Are you done yet?" asked Betsy. "I look out and you're either rolling up wire or laying it down. I think to myself, *The man has gone crazy. How do I stop him?*"

"I think so, for now anyway," I replied. Then I continued, "I do still have a lot of wire left."

We stayed with that configuration for a couple of weeks or so.

Then I thought, *Do we have enough wire to go around the pond?*

"Pretty darned close," I answered myself.

To elaborate, we don't have a pond. We have a *dream* of where we *want* a pond. We have even seen old maps showing where a pond used to be 130 years ago. But the reality is that we don't have a pond. If we do ever have the pond we want, it will cover about two to three acres. Again, we like to think big.

The next thing I knew, I was out fussing with the wire again. I had developed a new method of rerouting wire. I no longer re-rolled the wire. For one thing, what I had to redo would not fit on any reel I had. And even if I had a big enough reel, it would be awfully heavy for me to manage. My new method consisted of breaking the wire at one spot, going to where I wanted to start the new section, pulling the wire along the ground, and re-laying the wire as I went. This was not a perfect system. Often, the wire would get hung up on tree roots, rocks, fallen branches—anything in the woods it could get stuck on, it would. Still, there were long stretches where everything went smoothly enough to make it the preferred method. And Betsy broke down and decided to help me, although at this point, she was pretty sure I just liked laying down wire, pulling it back up, and laying it down again, creating a new, ever bigger enclosure.

"I can take it up the bank, back along the edge of the woods, through the field, and cross the stream at the driveway. I'll run it up the driveway and splice in where the wire crosses the driveway into the gravel bed."

Did I mention what a cruel thing it is to run your invisible fencing across your driveway? Our dogs like to go with us, and we enjoy taking them. However, the radio signal will penetrate a car's floor. You're supposed to remove the radio collars before you put the dogs in the car. We remembered about fifty percent of the time. The other fifty percent, you could hear a "yip, yip—Darned, I forgot to take the collars off," as we headed down our driveway.

Betsy's help was essential in finishing this last leg. In many ways, it was the hardest. Going through the field meant going through briar bushes, old juniper bushes, and even a clump of small thorn-apple trees. To boot, I ended up about fifty feet short of wire. Back to the lumberyard for one last roll.

Now we had arrived. I was done doing wire. If the dogs weren't happy with ten acres, so be it.

I should also mention that each time we changed configuration, it did upset the dogs, especially Bayley. Each time he came to the old wire border, he had to sniff and sniff. Even then, we frequently had to encourage him to wander farther. Spirit, on the other hand, seemed to take it in stride. One little sniff and a look around, and she was fine.

All in all, for a pretty reasonable price, we were able to enclose about ten acres. That was the spring of 1998. Every morning, Betsy, Bayley, Spirit, and I would take a walk around a trail inside the fence, and along our stream. It was about a quarter-mile long.

There was only one small problem: Invisible fencing works great with Border Collies, but not so great with Huskies. Occasionally, Spirit would bounce across the line just to see what was happening. Unfortunately, when Neeka arrived, she learned this bad habit. The problem is twofold. First of all, the fur around a Husky's neck is so thick that it's hard to get a good contact between the neck and the collar. Secondly, Huskies love to explore, and once in a while figure that the little "hit" they get from the collar is worth it just to see what's on the other side. The other problem we had was that we weren't able to block the muddy sections out of the fence. In fact, by adding the pond area, we opened a whole new mud area for the dogs to play in.

And we're not talking about mud-puddle mud. We're talking about deep, up-to-the-belly mud holes. For some reason, the dogs loved these things. It was not unusual on a dry, sunny day to have three dogs at the back door, absolutely filthy from the tummy down. Trying to keep the house clean, especially with wall-to-wall carpeting, was beginning to drive my wife crazy. Did I mention that our carpet was off-white? With the dogs, it became even further "off." Sometimes you wonder how you come to such decisions. I'm talking about that almost-white rug we had put in. It would eventually lead to two decisions, one good and one bad, but I'll get to those later.

We were fortunate in one way. Spirit never went very far. When she did escape, usually taking Neeka with her, she first went to the neighbor's house, a pretty little log cabin that sits about 150 to 200 feet or so back from the road. From there, they would go to the back of our house to Little Sandy Creek and play in the stream for a while before coming home. This trip took anywhere from one to two hours and drove us crazy. We would call and call, but the truth was that they wouldn't come home before they were good and ready. Luckily, our neighbors really liked our dogs. Mr. Smith especially liked Neeka. When I went looking for the dogs, I always went to his place first. It seemed the story was always the same.

"Yep. They were here about five, ten minutes ago. Hung around for a while, then headed off. I tell you, though, you better keep your eye on that red one. She's awful pretty, and somebody's gonna take off with her."

That was certainly a concern. Some Huskies will go off with anybody. The other concern was that some person would mistake her for a deer and shoot her. As we know, that is all too distinct a possibility around here.

We tried a couple of different interventions. The first was to shave a small spot on the neck for better connection. This worked a bit. The problem was that the collar frequently rotated away from where we had shaved the neck, negating any usefulness. The second intervention was to buy a more powerful collar. This worked okay but was anything but foolproof. Still, overall, this system worked better than any we had tried before, and we did have a fair amount of time and money invested. Not to mention the fact that it looked a whole lot better than the regular fencing that had stood for too many years.

Our solution, though not a great one, was to run with the dogs on a leash in the morning, and hope that it tired them out enough to just lay around inside the enclosure for the rest of the day. It worked great for the Border Collies. Neither Bayley nor Puzzles nor Crescent roamed, which was something given their history. They seriously respected the invisible fence, for which we were very thankful. In fact, it was so effective with them that all we had to do was set up some white warning flags and the Borders would not cross. After we put in the invisible fencing, they were very suspicious of anything white that was dangling, like my underwear on the clothesline. They were not about to get zapped twice.

Acquiring Neeka did have an unexpected result. As we got into fall, and Neeka got bigger and stronger, a miraculous thing happened. After seeing Neeka's "Huskiness," Spirit started to act more like a Husky herself. She began to smile that Husky smile. It looked like that mysterious ailment she had was depression. Bayley had brought her a little out of her depression, but it took another Husky to bring her out of it completely. The great thing is, not only did her overall attitude change, but Neeka's natural tendency to pull began to rub off on Spirit. It wasn't long before we had two pulling Huskies. What Karen had told us paid off. "Be patient, and she'll come around." With Neeka's help, she did. Now my wife had a team. I had two smiling Huskies and one smiling wife.

Chapter 7

The Training Cart

Somewhere along the way, before we acquired Neeka, we (mainly Betsy) decided that we needed a training cart. I don't remember if it was an original idea, or if we saw one in a catalog. In off-season training, when there was no snow, we had the dogs pull us on roller blades. This worked well but required a hard surface, and the dogs did not have to work much.

"It would give us more flexibility," she pointed out. "I bet with a cart we could go on dirt roads."

As she was saying this, she sort of snuggled up to me, got real close, and looked me straight in the eye. I knew that any objection I had would not make a difference, but I continued anyway.

"And just where do you plan on getting one of these carts?"

"I thought we'd make it."

"Let me think about it."

My family thinks I can make anything. I was still skeptical, but I was already beginning to think of how I might do it. My concept was to make the frame from aluminum tubing, preferably aircraft grade. This would make it light and strong. For wheels, I would use twenty-inch BMX bicycle wheels. I believed that this would make it more stable and give it a little better ride. For brakes, I would mount standard bicycle brakes on the steering mechanism.

Though I would have preferred a four-wheeled version, a three-wheeled would be much easier to build because of the steering mechanism. The biggest problem I had was how to mount the driver's riding deck. It needed to be only four or five inches off the ground to create a low center of gravity. If I put it in front of the rear axle, it would make it more stable, but much more dangerous in a rollover. Putting it behind the rear axle would mean too much weight in the back. The best solution for me, the brilliant non-engineer, was to make an offset axle that would hang down from the wheels. There were other details, but I figured if I could work out the big ones, the little ones would fall into place.

I explained my concept to Betsy. "What do you think?"

"Sounds good, but where are you going get all that stuff?"

"I haven't worked out all the details yet, but—"

"Hey!" she interrupted. "I bet my father could help."

Betsy's dad. His name is Ernest Balch, but he prefers to be called Ernie. In fact, he says that if you call him Mr. Balch, he'll think you're talking to his father. He was born in England in 1911. As of this writing, in his mid-nineties, Ernie shows no signs of slowing down. He is one of the kindest, gentlest, most generous people on the face of the earth.

He's also been described as either crazy, eccentric, or brilliant. He takes "do-it-yourself" to a higher level. One of the themes that runs through his work is fire safety. As a boy, most of the small town where he lived burned down. Though he was not in any real danger, he remembers visiting the village shortly after the fire. The image that stands out in his mind is glass melted on the street.

"The fire was so hot that the widows melted. I can still see it in my mind just as plain as day," he's told us. "I've never seen anything like it."

His need to build fireproof things was reflected in the construction of his garage. He built it himself. The walls are poured concrete. He was concerned how a concrete garage would look, so when he made the forms, he designed them so the finished product would look like clapboard siding. It worked. It was years before I found out the walls were concrete.

He also used concrete in building his house. The walls and roof are traditional construction, but the floors are concrete. The other thing that fascinates me is the heating system. It's in-floor hot-water heating. He built this system back in the late forties. The man was years ahead of the rest of us. Today, this system uses a special concrete mixture poured over a network of special plastic tubing. I believe my father-in-law used copper tubing and regular concrete. I don't know how he solved the problem of expansion and contraction of the tubing, but fifty years later, there are still no cracks in the floor, and the boiler, which was bought secondhand in the 1940s, still works.

Then there's our fireplace that he designed and built. He was a mere seventy-eight when he did this. It sits on four eighteen-square-inch concrete pillars, which support a concrete pad, which supports not only the fireplace, but also the chimney (which is—you guessed it—concrete).

"I don't trust cinder blocks. They crack too easily," he told me.

There are two chimneys. He built one for the main part of the house and one for the basement in case we needed it later. I remember plain as day him pouring the concrete.

Ernie mixed the cement, which we both hauled to the forms until it got too high to reach. At that point, we recruited Betsy's younger brother, Don, to help us. I lifted it up to Don, and he dumped it in. This part of the project took several days, since we could go up only a few feet at a time. Ernie, of course, made the forms. After all, he was the only one who knew what he was doing.

At the time, we didn't have a fully finished basement, but it would be harder to add a chimney when we put in the basement. He also designed the firebox, which was to be built of steel. He borrowed the design from an article he had read on old fireplaces. To see if it worked, however, he built a cardboard mockup, and set it where the finished product would go. A friend of ours just happened to be visiting.

"I can't believe this," he said, shaking his head. "This is amazing. I can tell you one thing, it's not going to fall down," he said as he looked at the massive pillars. He turned to Betsy's father. "Now, how exactly is this going to work?"

My father-in-law started to explain, then cut himself short. "Here. Let me show you."

Andy stared in disbelief as Ernie lit a small piece of paper and placed it in the center of the cardboard firebox.

"We'll see if the draw is any good" (meaning the smoke should go up the chimney instead of out into the room).

"Aren't you afraid of setting the cardboard on fire?" Andy asked.

"Oh no. The combustion temperature of the paper is lower than that of the cardboard," he answered matter-of-factly.

As the paper burned (it was only a few seconds), the smoke went up and out the mockup firebox. The transition piece from the firebox to the chimney was not yet in place.

Ernie gave out a little laugh, "Heh, heh. By golly, I think we got something here that's gonna work."

Andy couldn't believe what he had just witnessed. He still talks about the fireplace Ernie built and the fire he set inside a cardboard structure to test it out.

I can just imagine, ten thousand years from now, the house will be long gone, but the fireplace and chimney will still be standing. Some archeologist will find it and theorize that it was probably used in some sort of religious sacrificial ritual. "Oh," he or she will say, "the poor maidens who lost their lives on this altar. How sad."

Just recently, we installed fake logs powered by propane. Now Ernie shakes his head a little and gives out a barely audible sigh every time he visits and looks at the fireplace. While it is a lot easier on us, it troubles him to see his fireplace burning with gas.

Ernie is not above using fake products himself, however. One of my personal favorites was when he decided to put face (Betsy and I refer to them as *fake*) bricks on the outside of his house. Actually, it was his third wife's house. Betsy's mother and Ernie's second wife had each died. He had moved out of the house he built, leaving it to his oldest son, and lived in his new wife's house until her death.

Face bricks are like real bricks, but only one-quarter to three-eighths of an inch thick. Many people have used them around prefabricated fireplaces or on decorative walls. Ernie wanted to side three-quarters of the house with them. He went to a local store to price them. The person at the store gave him the price per box.

"Oh boy," he said in disbelief. "That works out to be about thirty cents a brick. I bet I could make them cheaper than that."

He then proceeded to work out the cost of materials. He could do it for ten cents a brick. Though most face brick is, I believe, made of a clay-based material, he would make his out of concrete. This presented a number of problems. First, he had to make a mold for the bricks. That was easy enough. He somehow made a brick mold that, when completed, left the *brick* with a finish that looked remarkably like a real brick. He could make approximately twenty bricks, give or take a few, in each lot.

Then, he had to figure a way for the face bricks to cure so they wouldn't crack. He solved this problem by building an oven that he ran at a low temperature. In the oven, he placed the bricks above a pan of water. This created a high-moisture environment that allowed the bricks to cure slowly and evenly, preventing cracking. He made one batch at a time, using different dyes for color variation. Now, he needed well over a thousand bricks for this project. This was not a do-it-in-a-week kind of deal. I think it strung out over a two-or-three-year period, but it got done. By the way, he was eighty-two or eighty-three when he started that project.

I'm only touching the surface of the things he's built or designed. He built his own sawmill. He built a one-quarter-size Dutch windmill. But my favorite project he completed when Betsy was still a young girl. It was one of his smaller projects. He looked at a cat litter scoop and thought, *I could make one of those.* And he did. He took about six or eight nails, welded them onto a little piece of round steel bar, and then welded that to an old large serving spoon handle. It wasn't pretty, but it worked—and as far as I know, it was used for as long as he had cats.

But back to the cart. Ernie had an idea, he said. A week or so later, he showed up at our house with a small-wheeled vehicle he had created. We loaded the dogs, the cart, and ourselves into the car and went over to the track at the fairgrounds. We hooked up Neeka and Spirit to the center post of the cart and planned to let Bayley run along the side of the contraption. Betsy stepped up on the little platform at the back, and they were off.

I'm not exactly sure what happened, but the next things I saw were Betsy flying through the air, the cart flipping over on its side, and the dogs slowing to a stop with a confused look on their faces. Betsy lay still for a minute as her dad and I rushed over. She had quite a road burn on her arms and knees, but she also had a smile on her face.

"What a rush," she said. "What a rush."

The thought of racing was still far from our minds. We just wanted to have fun. We still enjoyed having the dogs pull us on our inline skates. Many people thought we were crazy. They're right, of course, but we didn't care. It was fun. Although we sometimes skated locally at the fairgrounds, the small roads were quite short, and we ended up going in circles.

One of our favorite places to skate was Onondaga Lake Park. This park has a paved road just for bikers, joggers, walkers, and, of course, skaters. The park has become so popular that they have added a path just for walkers as a safety measure. What it's really known for, however, is as a place where inline skaters can have a great skate. It's approximately four miles roundtrip with a little quasi-fast-food stand at one end. You skate out; get a hot dog or burger, fries, and something to drink; then head back. When we take the dogs, we usually just get something to drink. It's much easier that way.

I have to admit that when we take the dogs, we get a lot of attention. Dogs pulling people on inline skates is not a common sight, at least yet, in spite of the fact that it is incredibly fun. True, there is an element of danger, but I'd rather be behind my dogs than bungee-jumping. At the time, Betsy would hook up Spirit and Neeka, and I would hook up Bayley. This was not nearly as much of a demand on Bayley as skiing, so we didn't really worry about him having to pull too hard and hurting his leg.

On one particularly glorious late summer day, we met our son Jeremy at the park. At the time, he was single, so he was inclined to occasionally do things with his parents. And he loved to skate. We had the dogs with us. This created a minor problem. You would think a dog for each person. That makes sense. Unfortunately, we had only two tug lines. Betsy decided that the solution was for her to take all three dogs (crazy lady). That way I could skate with my son.

We hooked up three antsy, hyper dogs to the tug line. This is not an easy task. Just when you think you have it, one of them twists or turns or steps over another dog's line. Finally, they were ready—Neeka on Betsy's left; Bayley in the middle, the lead position; and Spirit on the right.

Betsy quietly spoke the command "let's go, let's go."

Woo! They surged ahead like they were late for a deadline. Betsy did all she could do just to hang on. It was quite a sight. With nothing holding them back, Huskies and Border Collies can reach speeds of twenty-five or more miles per hour during their initial spurt. And with three dogs pulling one small person on skates, there was not much holding them back.

"You know we'll never catch her, don't you?"

"Maybe, but I'm gonna try."

Jeremy is a very good skater, but I still didn't give him much of a chance.

Off he went. I was right behind him. However, before I got very far, I met an old friend. We had worked together at Onondaga Music Service in Syracuse in the days when it was still a cozy little business.

"Hi, Randy. Did you see three dogs and my wife go by?"

Randy instantly perked up.

"I thought I knew that person," he said, a bit surprised. "Yeah! She was going like a bat outta hell!"

"That's her," I said.

"Yeah. At first, I thought 'that lady's gotta be crazy.' Then I thought 'she looks awfully familiar,' but I couldn't place her."

We exchanged a little more small talk, then said our goodbyes.

I took off after my wife and Jeremy. As I predicted, Jeremy soon realized that chasing after his mother was futile, and he came back to skate with me. To be perfectly honest, it wouldn't have surprised me to find the whole lot of them tangled around a tree—or worse, a bunch of other people. I started to picture this pile of skaters, bikers, women with babies in strollers, all piled up in the middle of the path. I shuttered. I skated on.

Nothing yet, I thought. *They must be doing okay.*

After about a mile or so, we saw Betsy headed toward us. She had gone almost to the other end and was coming back to get us.

"How'd it go?" I asked her. It certainly must have gone a lot better than I had imagined.

"Great! Though I did have a couple of little scares."

"What happened?"

"Well, we were flying, I mean flying, when a squirrel ran across in front of us."

"Oh no!"

"It turned out okay, though. There were a lot of people around, and when they saw the squirrel, they let out a collective gasp each with their vision of what would happen next. It was pretty funny. I could hear them gasp because they all did it together. I'm sure they all expected the dogs to give chase. Frankly, it crossed my mind, too. I shouted, 'On by!' and, by golly, they 'on byed.' Sure made me happy. Spirit gave a look, but that was all."

"Neeka was good, then?"

Neeka was young and still had that youthful, enthusiastic curiosity that occasionally led her off task.

"Yeah. She was great, but I don't think she even saw it."

"You kept going?" Jeremy said in near disbelief.

"Couldn't stop if I wanted too."

Boy, is this true, especially on inline skates. On skis, on relatively soft snow, going uphill, you might have a chance of not doing significant bodily harm to yourself, but usually the best choice is to hang on and hope for the best.

"Did you have any trouble with the signposts or anything else along the side?" I know that the Huskies don't like to run on pavement, so they pull off to the side on the grass. If the momentum is right, sometimes you're beside them, rather than behind them.

"No. They were great. Every time we came to something, Spirit went to the inside of it. Once she started around to the wrong side, but she corrected herself."

Another prime example of the Huskies' trail-following ability.

We turned the dogs around again and continued to the little food stand. After watering the dogs, the three of us got something to drink. We rested for a brief time, then headed back. Partway back, Betsy decided to share her dogs.

For whatever reason, I had brought the extra tug line and leashes for the dogs in a daypack. Anyway, even though we didn't have a tug line for Jeremy, we decided that because the dogs were a little tired and not apt to burst off the line like they do when they're fresh, he would be okay. Jeremy took Spirit. He's always really liked her. We hooked two leashes together to approximate the length of a tug line and hooked Jeremy and Spirit up. I took Bayley and Betsy took Neeka. Off we went.

"Whadda ya think?" I yelled to Jeremy as we glided along.

"This is great!" he responded.

"It is kind of a neat feeling, isn't it?" his mother asked.

Now Jeremy understands our love of the sport. There is just something about being connected to and working with dogs. I don't know what it is. Maybe it's the connection to the past. Northern Scandinavians have been doing this little-known sport for centuries (though reindeer and, in some cases, horses were used).

That's part of it, but it's much more than this, I think. It's the bond that develops. To see them pulling their little hearts out for you is uplifting. And they act like you're doing them the favor. I don't mean to romanticize this too much, but it is more than a fast ride. If that was all I wanted, I could buy myself a snowmobile. Yet I have no interest in owning one. I—we—like our dogs. They make us laugh, they make us cry, and they occasionally make us frustrated.

Just like kids. The only difference is that I don't have to put the dogs through college. And my kids, who are all grown and moved out, have always refused to pull us on skis.

But not all training went that smoothly. Take the time on Cape Cod. It was February 1998, though you wouldn't know it by the weather we were enjoying. It was the middle of an extended thaw—a sunny day, temperatures in the mid to upper sixties. Much like the day at Onondaga Lake Park. We were visiting our daughter, Amy, who had moved out of our area for a new job. Betsy and I decided that it would be a great time to take the dogs out for a skate.

Now, for those of you who aren't familiar with Cape Cod, it has what is known as the Rail Trail. It's an old railroad bed that winds thirty or so miles on the lower Cape (that's basically the eastern and central part). Since the Cape is nothing but a big sand bar, the trail has been paved to make it usable for bikes and now inline skates. It's also used by joggers and walkers. It's much like Onondaga Lake Park, but longer, narrower, and not in quite as good shape. And since it is thirty miles long, it crosses a number of public highways.

We arrived at one of the many entry points. There were several within a few minutes of Amy's. The original plan was to take Amy, with Puzzles and Crescent, with us. Unfortunately, Amy had hurt her ankle and was not able to go.

"Could you still take Puzzles and Crescent? They really need the exercise," she pleaded. Puzzles was beginning to get a little chunky.

"Sure. We planned to take them whether you went or not," said Betsy. "Dad can take the three Borders, and I'll take my Huskies."

I thought to myself, *A three-dog hookup again. Hmmm. But these are three Border Collies. That should be okay.*

Upon arrival, we all got out of the Subaru. Sometimes I think we must look like one of those little clown cars at the circus as five dogs clamored out. We got the appropriate tug lines. We still didn't have the right setup for three dogs, but we were able to make do. The only potential problem was that we had only two necklines. Necklines run from the collar of one dog to the one next to it. This keeps the dogs close together, though my wife and I usually butt-line them, connecting them together at the end of the harnesses.

With only two necklines, one Border, Bayley as it turned out, had to be on a single line. I didn't worry a lot about it. When these three run together, they run together—tight, shoulder to shoulder. Crescent on the left, Puzzles in the middle, and Bayley on the right. You couldn't slip a sheet of paper between them. It's pretty neat to see, really. Anyway, Betsy got her two hooked up before me.

"Can I go?" she asked. "They're really antsy."

"Yeah. I'm almost ready, and they're being pretty good." That was a surprise, but they were behaving.

"Okay. Let's go." And off they flew.

"Easy guys. Easy," I pleaded. "Just let me get on my feet."

They had been good until now. But they didn't like being left behind. I managed to get up and yell "Hike, hike." I was still using the old commands, unlike my wife. We were on our way. Betsy was only a few yards ahead of us.

"Woo! Good dogs." As predicted, they were shoulder to shoulder. *No problem*, I thought. *This is great.*

We sailed along. Betsy and her strong Huskies were gradually pulling away from us. There weren't too many other people on the trail. This in stark contrast to summer, when the trail is very busy. But this was February, when there are not many people around. It was not, however, deserted.

I looked ahead and saw a little old lady walking toward us from the opposite direction. As Betsy approached her, I saw the nice little old lady give a smile and a nod to Betsy and her team. I'm sure the lady was thinking, *How cute.* By now, Betsy and her team were about 100 yards ahead of us. My team and I were quickly coming up on the nice little old lady.

When she was near, I gave the command, "Over Gee! Over Gee!"

I gave a tug on the line. The Borders moved, but not quite in the right directions. Puzzles and Crescent moved over to the left, and Bayley and his tug line moved over to the right. I can still see it now.

We're gonna clip that lady right off at the knees, I thought. I looked up at the little old lady. Her friendly smile had turned into a look of sheer terror.

I figured my only chance of saving the poor lady was to go off to the left and give a hearty tug, hoping that I could pull Bayley over with me. To do this, I would likely run into a tree that was right in my potential path. I thought, I'll put my wrist guards up and hit the tree, cushioning the blow with my arms. Okay. It may not have been a great plan, but I didn't have a lot of time. As soon as I hit the side of the trail and the sand, I went flying.

I did hit a tree, but not quite in the manner in which I had planned. The trees in this spot were more like large twigs. Too small to cushion my wrist guards, but big enough to do some damage. My hands slipped off a trunk. Then, THUMP! I hit the tree with my chest. I then skidded off to the side and ended up flat on my face. Fortunately, I was wearing all of my safety equipment. I'm not *that* stupid.

As I lay there, I heard a small voice ask, "Are you all right?"

It was the little old lady, still standing. My plan, though not perfect, had worked.

"Yeah. I think so."

"Are you sure?"

"Yeah. I'm fine. Just a few bumps." What a trooper I am.

"Okay." She turned and walked away. Well, it wasn't pretty, but I had managed to keep her upright. That made me feel pretty darned good.

As I was getting up off the ground to assess the damage, Betsy and her Huskies came back to get me.

"Is she all right?" Betsy asked.

That wasn't the question I expected. "Is *she* all right? What about me?" I asked with disbelief, a little peeved.

"Didn't you see what happened?"

"I was otherwise occupied, you know." Perhaps she didn't notice that I was covered with sand from head to toe.

"You knocked that little old lady down."

"What?" I said incredulously.

"Yeah. I turned around just in time to see Bayley knock her down."

So, let's get this straight, I thought. What I had done was pull Bayley into the little old lady. He caught one of her legs, she did a 180 and landed on her back. I just couldn't believe it. I had really thought my great plan had worked.

"The only thing I remember is her coming over and asking me how I was."

"You didn't ask her how *she* was?" Betsy asked, seeming a little upset.

"No," I said. I still couldn't believe that she had also fallen. "By the time I knew what was happening, she was already up. Aren't you a little curious as to how I am?"

"I'm sorry, hon," her tone much softer now. "How are you, anyway?"

"Just a few bumps, and I ate a little sand. That's all. All this stuff," motioning to my wrist, elbow, and knee guards and helmet, "worked just like it was supposed to."

"You want to keep going, or should we go back?"

"I'd just as soon go back. I've had enough excitement for one day."

We got all of our dogs in the right order and headed back. They had been waiting very patiently. Dogs, at least these dogs, seem to know when something had gone wrong, and they become incredibly well-behaved.

When we got to the car and took off all of our equipment, we did a preliminary exam of my body. I exposed as much of myself as was decent. As I'd thought, just a few bumps, bruises, and scrapes.

As I think back on it, I realize that she really was a nice little old lady. In spite of her fall, which was totally not her fault, she was genuinely concerned about me. When she asked me how I was, there was a gentleness in her voice. That's why I didn't believe I knocked her down. There's a lot of good people in the world, and she is one of them. Thanks, little old lady.

Chapter 8

We Still Need Another Dog

Three dogs are just not enough. As you may recall, this all began when we decided that Bayley was just not strong enough to pull Betsy on her skis on his own. We then added Spirit to help him. Unfortunately, Spirit did not seem too interested in pulling either. We purchased Neeka. She appeared to bring out the "Husky-ness" in Spirit and the need for a leader in Bayley. Betsy now had a three-dog team, though still rough around the edges, that would whisk her through the woods at breathtaking speed.

There was only one small problem. No matter how hard I might try, now there was no way I could keep up. Remember that the whole point of having a dog or dogs pull Betsy was so *she* could keep up with *me*. We had now come 180 degrees. Plan B: I will take Bayley, I thought. We'll work together, him pulling as much as his leg will allow, and me skiing as hard as I can—which is the way I like to ski. This worked pretty well. Off the Huskies and Betsy would go, flying like the wind, smooth and powerful. Off Bayley and I would go, Bayley with his head down, determined, and me, poles and skis flailing, nearly keeping up. This system worked pretty well for a couple of weeks.

After 500 meters or so, all the dogs would settle into a slow lope. Also, one of the reasons Bayley and I could keep up was because the Huskies, especially Neeka, were easily distracted and would periodically slow to check out their surroundings.

Then Amy visited with her two Border Collies.

It was Sunday, the day after Tourathon day. The Tug Hill Tourathon is a fifty kilometer (about thirty-one miles) cross-country ski race held annually about ten minutes from our house. The original plan was for Amy to take her two Borders, Puzzles and Crescent; I would take Bayley; and of course, Betsy would take Spirit and Neeka. Unfortunately, Amy got sick. Therefore, I ended up with a three-Border team.

The day was crisp and beautiful. Though one Border Collie may pull adequately, three Borders are very powerful. And their work ethic is unmatched. The Borders and Huskies just kept egging each other on. And since it was a beautiful Sunday afternoon, there were lots of people on the trails. When the teams collectively slowed a little bit, a group of skiers would appear over the horizon, exciting the dogs, and the chase was on once again.

"On by, on by!" we shouted, "On by!"

The dogs were much more interested in seeing what was just over the hill, so while they might give a quick look as we came upon slower skiers, they would pass by easily, slowing a bit until they would see something new on the horizon. I'm sure you're wondering what happens when you meet another dog. This was slightly more of a problem, and somewhat unpredictable. If the other dog did not directly interfere, ours would run right by. But the fear was another dog would attack one of ours.

All the dogs we met that day, though, were with someone that made it a little easier. As soon as we noticed the dog,

Gary and Jeremy at Tourathon Finish

we would yell, "Get your dog!" It's amazing how quickly people respond when five dogs and two skiers are barreling down
on them full tilt. One person responded, "It's not my dog!" to
which we responded, "Grab it anyway!" She did.

When we finished the run that day, I had a smile on my
face that I couldn't hide from my wife. For the first time, I
felt what my wife had been experiencing all those years with
Leo and then with Bayley, Spirit, and Neeka. The exhilaration
is nearly indescribable. It's not just going fast on your skis,
although that certainly is a part of it. It's being with your dogs,
doing what you love to do, doing what they love to do. There
is a joy, a rush, that is hard to match. Don't get me wrong.

I still love to cross-country ski strictly under my own power, but I knew I was hooked on skijoring now. I had to have a team. Betsy knew that I had to have a team. It was time to consider our options.

Option one: I could take Bayley and Spirit, and Betsy could take Neeka. This, in many ways, made the most sense. It was now clear that Neeka would be plenty strong enough to pull my wife. At only nine months of age, she was already frequently doing at least half, usually more, of the pulling. She was developing that Husky look when she pulled; it's a lot like watching a horse run. The head thrusts forward, reaching, reaching; the tongue (I swear Huskies have the longest tongue for their size of any animal) frequently dangling to one side. I love just watching them run.

Borders, on the other hand, have a different look. It's a look of sheer determination and all business. When Borders are playing, they look playful, bouncing about with a *joie de vivre* that lifts the soul. When they're working, however, it's a different story. Work hard, play hard—that's a Border Collie. The head goes down and forward, and the Border Collie focus sets in.

I doubt that there is any breed of dog that can focus better than a Border. Sometimes it's a little scary. All attention is directed, in this case, at pulling toward some unseen goal. They don't care why; they don't question (unless the master gives what appears to be a really stupid command, like yelling "Gee" (right) when the trail obviously goes "haw" (left). The Border runs smoothly. I swear you could put a glass of water on its back, and it would never spill a drop.

As I said, that option made the most sense. We knew the dogs, they knew us. We were only recently a family that even considered having more than one dog. More than *three*? This seemed a scary proposition.

But Betsy and I came up with a few rationalizations to discard option one. How long could we expect Bayley to pull, given his two questionable legs? Aren't we being unfair to the poor little guy? Will Spirit ever be a consistent puller, given her bouts of depression? Maybe she has a health problem that slows her down, given her extremely quiet nature. Reason after reason came streaming forth as to why we needed another dog, maybe even two if I wanted an all-Border-Collie team. The truth is, Betsy didn't want to give up a dog, especially Spirit, and I wanted to go faster and farther. It seemed that once we moved past the idea of having only one dog, we simply went right over an edge.

Option two: Acquire another dog. Are we crazy? Well, yes, we are. So we made the decision to get another dog. Our first impulse was to get another Husky. Our reasoning was that a good, strong Husky would do seventy to ninety percent of the pulling, taking a lot of pressure off Bayley. We bought a copy of *The Swap Sheet*, a newspaper containing only classified ads, and the Sunday paper. The search was on.

We opened the *The Swap Sheet* and started in scanning through the pets' section. There it was:

Purebred Siberian Husky. One year old, red and white.
$150.

This was great. A young dog, but one that was already housebroken. He could also pull immediately—maybe. We also checked the Sunday paper. There were several more ads for Huskies, but all were for puppies. We didn't particularly want a puppy, for two reasons. First, we were still finishing all that puppy stuff with Neeka, who was only nine months old. Second, a puppy purchased now would not be able to skijor this season at all. We decided to call on the yearling Husky.

Betsy made the call. The dog was an AKC-registered, unaltered male, fifteen months old. This had some appeal. We had not decided whether to breed Neeka. If this dog had the right characteristics, and the bloodlines didn't cross with Neeka's, the potential for beautiful, hard-working dogs was high.

"Why are you selling the dog?" Betsy queried.

You always wonder why someone wants to get rid of a dog after they've had it for more than a year. Most of the reasons that pop into one's head aren't good ones. Bad behavior, some health defect, the dog wouldn't housebreak, it barks all the time, it pees on your leg—these are just some of the possibilities that flashed through my mind.

"I just got laid off, and I need the money," came the response from the other end.

I didn't find this to be very comforting. I imagined two possible scenarios. One, the person never cared much for the dog, just marginally cared for it, and thus the dog was more of a burden that it was worth. Or two, he really did care about the dog, was selling it out of desperation, and, after agreeing to sell it to us, would run after us as we were pulling out of his driveway yelling "Wait! Wait! I've changed my mind!" I didn't want to deal with either one. I didn't want to fall in love with a dog and have it snatched back.

But Betsy wrote down the directions, and we agreed to meet. The directions to the house seemed more complex than they ultimately turned out to be.

"We'll be coming down from Sandy Creek on Route 81," my wife informed him.

140

"Okay. Get off at the Parish exit. Turn left onto Route 49."

"Don't you mean Route 69?" my wife asked.

"Yeah, I guess. It's one of those. Do you know where County Route 11 is?"

"No."

"Do you know where the Grist Mill is?" (The Grist Mill is a big truck stop just off I-81. It's open twenty-four hours a day, seven days a week, and is a good place to stop for pie.)

"Yes," Betsy replied, feeling a little encouraged.

"It's not that road."

That's good. Now at least we know where he isn't.

"It's the next road on the right, up about a half mile. We're the first mobile home on the right, about three and a half miles down the road. You can't miss us. There's a horse in the front yard."

This conjured up some interesting images. This part of upstate New York can be pretty rural. I could just see it. A horse in the front, maybe a cow and a couple goats in the back, chickens running around all over the place. Eight kids, all under the age of five, running around barefoot in the snow. It's amazing the images that flash through your mind. It also makes me a little nervous when someone says, "You can't miss it." I not only can, but I have.

The next day we started down Route 81. We got off in Parish and turned left onto route whatever, went about a half mile and turned right onto County Route 11. That was easy enough. It's curious how far three and a half miles is when you're looking for something. Finally, after what seemed more like thirty miles, sure that we had indeed missed it, I saw it—a horse in the front yard.

Next, I saw the Husky. Unfortunately, we had passed by the driveway. I don't know if that counts as missing it or not;

you decide. We turned around and drove in. As is usually the case, my images were not very accurate. There were other animals—three beautiful Dalmatian puppies and a three-legged Border Collie. A man, probably in his mid to late thirties, came out to greet us.

"Well, there he is. His name is Ricky."

Oh no. A human name.

He pointed to a beautiful red and white Husky. He was lying on top of his doghouse. This is typical for Huskies. If you're considering owning a Husky, a doghouse with a flat roof would be greatly appreciated by the dog. When he noticed us, he jumped off his doghouse and began leaping straight up and down with excitement. This is also typical behavior for Huskies.

You can just see their joy for life, their mountainous energy, their power, and best of all, their "I'm so glad you came to visit to me"-ness. It's really pretty neat. There are few creatures in this world that make you feel more welcome than a Husky. He had a short nose (Neeka's is ridiculously long) and the type of face that looks like he's wearing a mask. He was a good-sized dog weighing in at about fifty-five pounds. My first thought was, *Boy, he and Neeka would have beautiful puppies.*

The big question, of course, is, will he run? Remember, we already have three dogs of uncertain ability—a Border Collie with a questionable leg, a moody Husky, and an enthusiastic but untried pup.

"He looks really good, but my wife and I need to think about it."

"No problem," said the man.

Betsy and I went back to the car to discuss the pros and cons. He certainly looked healthy. And the way he leaped about, he appeared to be strong enough. But would he run? There's only one way to find that out. We got out of the car and went back to the man.

"We'd like to try him out, if that's okay. We need to make sure that he will get along with the other dogs and make sure he wants to pull."

"That'd be fine."

"We'll give you a check," Betsy said. "If we bring him back, you can just give me back the check."

"Great," said the man.

"Who do I make the check out to?"

I suddenly realized that we had been doing all this transacting, and nobody knew who they were talking to. We had all been too focused on the dog.

"Keith Jenkins," responded the no-longer-nameless man.

"Is it okay if we pick him up tomorrow?" Betsy asked.

"No problem. I'll be here," responded Keith.

We went home, still pondering the merits. Our first concern was whether we could change his name without totally disrupting his psyche. I finally came up with Brick. I'm sure there are many of you reading this who think Brick is not much of an improvement, but it's the best I could do on such short notice. As soon as we got home, we arranged with our local vet to check out Brick/Ricky the next morning.

When the next morning arrived, we called Keith to let him know when we would be picking up the dog. We wanted to time it so we could stop at the vet on the way home.

"We'd like to pick Brick up about 10:30," I said.

When Betsy heard this, she started waving hysterically at me. "The dog's name is Ricky," she mouthed.

Oops.

"Okay. We'll be here," came Keith's wife's voice from the other end. I don't think she noticed my blooper.

We picked up Ricky and headed to the vet. The doctor didn't find any obvious defects, and we continued home. The next step was meeting our other dogs. We took him to the dog pen and introduced him. Spirit was ecstatic. It was like she had been reunited with a long-lost love. She leaped about and had about as big a Husky smile as I've ever seen. Bayley seemed excited to have a new playmate as well. But Ricky's attention was centered on our unspayed, ten-month-old pup, Neeka. As soon as he saw her, he had one thing on his mind. Fortunately, Neeka was not in heat, so it was a platonic re-lationship, but no doubt about it, Ricky had charisma, and Neeka was noticing him, too.

But for the big test—will he pull?

Once we got Neeka and Ricky to focus on something other than each other, we loaded the dogs in the car and headed off to the trails. We harnessed them up, Betsy with Neeka and Spirit, and Ricky and Bayley with me. Neeka and Spirit took off. Bayley did the skijor dog lunge. Ricky stood still. Betsy went a little way and turned her team around when she noticed I wasn't behind her. Ricky was asking to get back in the car. We coaxed a bit. Bayley licked Ricky's face. Neeka and Spirit danced around, wanting to get going again.

Now, we know that you can actually *train* dogs to pull, but up to this point, training a dog to pull was never neces-sary. They just plain *wanted* to pull. Ricky, even with other dogs around him encouraging him to pull, simply sat down. He was a sweet dog. He got along with our dogs. But he wasn't the dog we were looking for. Sadly, we returned Ricky to his owner, and the search continued.

Chapter 9

How Can It Be So Hard to Find the Right Dog?

Betsy and I talked. Maybe it wasn't a Husky that we wanted. Maybe what we needed was another Border Collie to run along with Bayley. We started looking in the newspaper again. We saw an ad:

Border collie. Six months old. Misshapen face. Call …

I made the call. The dog was located about forty miles from our house.

Ted answered. "He's a really nice dog, but he was injured accidentally by his mother just after he was born, and his top and bottom jaw no longer line up. Otherwise he is a healthy dog. It's just that no one wants to buy him. I will give you a good deal."

We got the directions and arranged to meet the dog the next day. The discussion had conjured up all kinds of images of the dog, and we both worried a bit, but if he was healthy, maybe he would be just the dog for us.

We drove slowly down the road, looking for the house number the owner had given us. There it was. We both stared.

145

There were broken-down cars littered throughout the yard. Several goats were tethered to posts. Ted met us and pointed to a building behind the house. As we walked toward the barn where we were to meet the young dog, another Border Collie sprang out of a car window with a loud, frightening bark and a deep growl. He was brought up short by a rope tied to his collar. Ted gestured to the dog to get back in the car, and he disappeared in through one of the windows.

I had an uneasy feeling about this place. More cars, more dogs fastened to them, and most didn't seem that friendly. Betsy gave me a quick look, eyes wide. We picked our way around the debris that seemed to lie everywhere and went into the barn.

"Here's the pup," the man said, seemingly unaware of the mess that was around him. "His mother rolled over on him a day or so after he was born and dislocated his jaw. It never healed right, and nobody wanted to buy him."

The dog eased himself behind a bale of hay and kept backing up. He growled. Just a little bit, but it was disconcerting. We squatted down and gently reached out our hands. The dog's hair stood up, and he backed up further. We backed off. I felt sorry for the pup, but was very uneasy about taking this little one home. We turned to the man, tried to smile in a friendly way, said we didn't think the dog was quite what we were looking for.

Then Betsy and I nearly tripped over each other trying to get back to our car. Dogs jumped from cars as we hurried across the yard. We jumped but tried not to break into a full-blown run. We climbed into our car, shocked into speechlessness. It had been a strange visit.

"I just didn't think it would be this hard to find a dog that would work for us," I said to Betsy. We were still skijoring.

Betsy with Spirit and Neeka, and Bayley and I chugging along as fast as I could. We talked. Yes, although our search hadn't gone very well so far, we decided we still wanted another dog. We needed a dog that would get along with our three dogs and that would enjoy pulling.

Aha—why didn't we think of this before? We realized we needed to talk with some of the local mushers and see if anyone had a dog that would be a good match for us. We decided to talk with someone that has a team to see if they had a dog we might buy. We asked around, and someone mentioned a husband and wife who raced Siberian Huskies. We got the number and gave a call.

"Hi," Betsy said when a man answered the phone. "We are just beginning to do some skijoring, and we are looking for a dog to add to our teams. We have two Siberian Huskies and a Border Collie right now and would like to find just the right dog to run with our Border Collie."

There was a short pause on the other end of the line, and then the man responded, "I might have just the dog for you."

I should probably point out that skijoring and dog sledding, while related, each require something a bit different from a dog. For one thing, in skijoring, you want a dog that is not afraid to lead. Some dogs simply feel too much stress when they are placed in a leadership position, while others seem to enjoy it. With a dog sled team, there are both leaders and followers. We needed a leader, and one that was not intimated when there was not a team behind him.

Second, you need a dog that will stop if you fall. This became extremely clear to my wife when a friend asked her to take a couple of his dogs skijoring to see how they would do. They were leaders. Fearless. And extremely strong. Betsy confidently hooked herself up to the two Alaskan Huskies while the owner held them reasonably still, and off she went at breathtaking speed. My wife has always loved speed, so there was a smile a mile wide as she disappeared over a rise in the trail.

Unfortunately, there was a sharp turn in the trail that Betsy had always navigated just fine (she wasn't as fast a skier as I was, but she was a more skilled one), and she was still smiling as she started to take the turn. At this increased speed, though, one ski turned quickly enough while the other didn't, and down she went, on her face. These dogs were used to pulling a sled, and they hardly seemed to feel my wife's fall. They continued to pull her along, face first, in the snow.

You might wonder why she didn't let go, but once you have been doing a little bit of dog sledding or skijoring, you quickly learn one of the most important and basic rules of running dogs—don't ever let go. And she didn't. For a long time. But finally, recognizing that the dogs were never going to stop, with great reluctance, she snapped the quick release on her belt, and the dogs shot away. She got up and began to ski back to the owner, worrying that she had lost his dogs. As she rounded the last bend, she was extremely relieved to see the two dogs had finished the loop and had returned.

Their owner, however, was worried when the two dogs returned dragging a tug line behind, with no skier attached. He looked up and saw a snow covered, weary skier; then there were two relieved humans, the dogs were still intact, and so was my wife, almost. So you see, in skijoring, it is best if you have a dog that will stop if you fall.

But I digress. We were still trying to find that fourth dog. The dogsledder we called knew that we would need a leader, and one that was a bit sensitive to what was behind him.

"I have a six-year-old that's a good leader. One of my other dogs, though, just doesn't like him and has been harassing him. I have been trying to decide what I should do about him. Maybe a new home would be just the thing."

"We'd like to see how he gets along with our other dogs, if that's okay," I said.

There was also a little concern about whether he would feel confident to lead without a team behind him.

"We are going to be away for the next week or so at some races," the dogsledder said. "Would you consider keeping him with your dogs for that long?"

It seemed the perfect solution. We had also planned on entering our first race the next weekend. "Would you mind if we took him to Canada for a race there?"

"No," our new friend answered. "That will give you a good idea if he will work out or not."

We drove the twenty or so miles to the dogsledder's house and picked up the dog, with the unlikely name of Norm. He was not beautiful. In fact, he was rather gangly, with patchy, short hair, but for reasons that are never easy to understand, my wife and Norm quickly bonded. Although Norm had never been in a house before, he climbed up onto the bed with the rest of the dogs, his head resting on Betsy's back.

Only two days after Norm came to temporarily live at our house, we left to try our hand at a dogsledding and skijoring race in Canada. We were excited and extremely nervous. We had been told that this event was a great one to try, as it was primarily designed just for fun. There would be some seasoned racers there to offer advice, and lots of newer people like us. We also knew that if we chickened out, we would just enjoy watching the others race.

We loaded the dogs. We loaded the equipment. And off we went. We had made arrangements to stay at the inaptly named Black Forest Schnitzel House and Motel. It was in the middle of nowhere and came complete with a junk car in the front yard. Attached to the motel was a little restaurant that appeared to cater to the locals. While many mushers have large trucks in which they leave their dogs, we had our little Subaru station wagon that satisfactorily held our four dogs. The motel owners allowed us to take all four dogs into our room for the night, and we all slept reasonably well.

The next morning was race day. We were excited. The dogs were also excited, as if they knew they were about to have a great, new adventure. We decided to start the day off by having breakfast in the restaurant and, as we did not want to leave the dogs unattended in the motel room, began to load them into the back of the station wagon, parked in the lot in front of the restaurant. Here, we figured, we could keep a watchful eye on them.

We were feeling pretty cool. We were racers. We had cool dogs. We were feeling ready.

Then something went terribly wrong. Somehow, Norm slipped his collar as we were about to load him, and he began joyfully bounding around the parking lot. On one side was the road (which, while not busy, was still worrying), and in the back of the motel was an

obvious snowmobile trail that went off to who knew where. Huskies, we had come to understand, seem to have an inner gene that tells them to run on a trail, in one direction, for miles, not always knowing how to return. We gasped. We didn't want Norm to head to the road or the trail.

My wife quickly loaded our other three dogs into the car. Unfortunately, in her haste to come help me try to capture Norm, she left the back gate up on the station wagon. Now *all* the dogs were running around the parking lot. Somehow, and with some effort, she managed to get our three dogs back inside the car and shut the door. Now we could both concentrate on Norm. We knew we were at considerable risk of losing a dog that didn't belong to us. Norm had not gotten his bearings yet and was still enjoying his brisk run around the parking lot.

My wife looked at Norm, who was heading in her general direction, a huge smile on his face. She did a quick calculation in her head: "If I time it perfectly, I can do this." She took a deep breath, launched herself into the air, and without trying to catch herself from falling, flattened poor Norm to the pavement. She held on to him around the neck while I quickly got his collar and leash on, and we got him safely into the car, apparently unscathed from his morning jaunt and being flattened by a human, no less. A huge, collective sigh came from both of us. Betsy brushed herself off. We resumed our air of cool dog racers and entered the restaurant.

What we had forgotten was that there were huge windows in the front of the restaurant, giving all the early breakfast patrons a full view of the parking lot. We quickly realized that we had provided considerable entertainment to all these early-morning customers. As we entered, people quickly shuffled back to their tables. The proprietor dryly, and with a marvelous Canadian lilt, commented, "Got your morning exercise, eh?"

I would like to say that things at this first race went up from there, but it would not be strictly true. We found our way to the race site and were glad we had an all-wheel-drive car. As with many race sites, this one was off the beaten track, on a marginally maintained road. We arrived and were immediately caught up in the excitement. There were trucks everywhere. Dogs were barking. People greeted us, and we signed in, paid our entry fee, and went back to let our dogs out of the car.

We looked around at the various methods others used to handle a large number of dogs. Most of the dogs were connected to wire lines that ran along each side of a dog truck, allowing the dogs a bit of room to move about and relieve themselves.

Betsy, Gary, Spirit, Neeka, Norm, and Bayley at their first race

Since we had only four dogs, we each walked with two dogs along the edge of the parking lot, with various success in getting them to go to the bathroom.

Before we left home, we had purchased four longish chains to connect to our Subaru so the dogs could be safely left out of the car for short periods of time. What we hadn't thought about, though, was that three of our dogs had never been chained, let alone to a car sitting in a parking lot full of hundreds of other dogs. They were used to a fenced-in yard and frequently coming and going inside the house. When we placed them on the chains connected to the car, they looked totally confused, and more than a little annoyed. They seemed to be telling us that they were not ordinary sled dogs and should not be treated as such. Norm, however, took his connection to the car in stride and simply laid down, perhaps resting after his morning run. And, anyway, he had done this many times.

We walked a bit around the parking lot, looking at the wide range of dogs that were to take part in the race. There were all sizes, shapes, and colors, although most were some kind of Husky mix. We were surprised, and pleased, to see a woman with several Border Collies, and learned that she races a purebred Border Collie team in the four-dog dogsledding. It was a bit unusual, but made it seem as though Bayley fit right in. Just how well became apparent rather quickly.

Somehow—and I simply, after all these years, don't remember how—Bayley managed to get free. We didn't notice immediately, and a few minutes had passed before we began our frantic calls.

"Bayley!" we hollered at the top of our lungs. "Where are you, boy?" "Bayley, come!" We called again and again.

We could not believe that he wasn't coming. He had nearly flawless recall and was often off leash when we went for a walk. We certainly had no intention of having him get free now, but still we expected him to come quickly when he heard us yelling his name. Our calls became increasingly frantic as we ran up and down the rows of trucks amid the din of barking dogs. He was nowhere. We continued to call, almost pleading with him to come to us.

As we made our way around the trucks, dogs, and people, a man came walking up to us.

"Are you missing a dog?" he asked.

"Yes," we both answered at once.

"Was it a Border Collie?" he continued.

"Yes!" Our heads were bobbing quickly up and down. Hope was surging in us.

"Someone found one a little bit ago." He said. "They thought he belonged to the woman who runs a Border Collie team here and tied him up to her truck."

We raced around the parking lot looking for the Border Collie lady. And there was her truck. Tied to it, along with four other dogs that looked very much like him, was a rather forlorn Bayley, straining to come to us. The owner of the other Borders was not at her truck, so probably never even noticed that her dog team had grown from four to five. We breathed a sigh of relief for the second time that day and walked, with Bayley, back to our car. We were all together again.

And the rest is history. We put on our bibs, proudly displaying our race numbers, and each stood at the race line in our turn.

And this is where this book began.

"5 – 4 – 3 – 2 – 1! Go driver!" yelled the timekeeper.

Gary, Betsy, and Spirit

"Hike! Hike! C'mon, Bayley! C'mon, Norm!" I shouted. With a jerk and a jump, we were off—me on skis, two dogs dragging a hapless human in their wake. I was thinking, *Oh please, please let me get around the first corner and out of sight before I fall.*

Fortunately, it's only about 200 meters to the first turn. My odds were good.

155

"Haw, Bayley! Haw, Norm!" We turned left and out of view.

"We made it. If I fall now, only one or two racers at most will see me," I say to myself. I'm very relieved. As I settle in behind the dogs, I look at the beauty around me. It is snowing, and I am part of the landscape.

Betsy and I did very well that day. Norm was perfect as he paced steadily alongside Bayley, who ran with heart and joy. I finished in second place and Betsy in third. It was a two-day race, but we had planned to race only on Saturday, just to get our feet wet in the sport. Our strong showing tempted us to stay on, but we had a borrowed dog and a long way to go home, so even though several of the other skijorers encouraged us to stay, we reluctantly loaded our dogs and began the return trip. I didn't know it at the time, but it was the last race I was ever to make.

Chapter 10

No, You Can't Name Him Ichabod

Betsy and Norm snuggled together on the way home, and we arrived tired but elated. We had successfully run our first race and, in addition, done better than we could have ever imagined. We thought we had our new dog and, although we had tried to lose two of them, we had managed to all end up back home. Norm's owners had encouraged us to take Norm to the vets' to be checked out before we purchased him, and the day after we arrived back home, we did just that.

Norm was a cooperative patient, and we waited for the test results to come back. The vet entered the room with very disappointing news.

"Norm is strongly heartworm positive," he said. "He will need a lengthy period of treatment and may never be strong enough to run with a team."

We both took a quick intake of breath, realizing that Norm had just run his heart out two days earlier.

"I know you are looking for a dog to add to your skijor teams, and I don't think Norm is that dog."

I looked quickly at Betsy and saw that she was fighting back tears. In retrospect, I have always wondered if we simply should have kept Norm and nursed him through the months of treatment, regardless of what the outcome was to be.

But we were in a different mindset then, and Norm went back to his team and his owners.

We had nearly given up looking for a new dog and were a comfortable family of two adults and three wonderful dogs. But we didn't completely give up. One day, Betsy was looking at the listings of dogs from our local shelter.

"Hey, Gar," she said. "They have a Husky available at the shelter. Should we go have a look?"

"Sure. It won't hurt to check it out."

Betsy, in a rare moment of elitism, announced, "Since we have two purebred Siberians, I am only interested if it is another purebred."

While she was not typically an elitist, she was bigtime into matching things, so I expect that played a role in her comment.

We drove the few miles to the shelter and entered a barn where several dogs were kept. We were led to a large, extremely skinny dog, who was clearly *not* a purebred. His legs were overly long, and his nose was enormous. With freckles on his face, he had an intriguing look about him. He was what many people refer to as an Alaskan Husky, and he looked like many of the dogs we had seen at the race.

The shelter worker said he thought the rescued dog might have been lost from a sled dog team, but they had called all the local sled dog people, and no one had lost a dog. He further explained that this dog had been eluding capture for several months and, even after the month he had been at the shelter, he still needed to gain a considerable amount of weight.

Betsy stepped in close to him, and I watched as this ungainly dog pressed his body firmly against Betsy's legs. I held my breath and then watched as she clipped a leash unto the dog, turned to the shelter person, and asked what the fee was.

I started to breathe again. I had already fallen in love with this dog. We paid the modest fee and walked away with the dog.

What happens next will sound like a made-up story, but every word is true. We drove home, and I casually watched as the new dog and Betsy rubbed heads together. Purebred only, indeed!

We still had Norm's harness, as we had forgotten to return it when we had taken Norm home. We planned to return it in the next day or so, but we were happy to have an extra harness to try on the new dog. First, though, we took the new dog out to the fenced-in yard to meet with our other dogs. The fence, which at this point was made up of several strings of electric wire, was unfamiliar to the new dog, but he was far more interested in introducing himself to his new family than in examining the fence. We fed them all some treats, and then brought the dogs into the house to harness them up and take them all out for a quick run.

As we got out the harness, the new dog came eagerly over and started to nose it. Then, unbelievably, he stepped into the harness, clearly having done this before. We had stumbled upon an experienced sled dog.

We'd opened the front door to take the dogs out to the car, when the new dog streaked out before we could stop him. At first, we tried to run after him, ineffectually calling out, "Here, dog! Come here, dog!" He had no name that we knew, and it was clear that this dog was fast and determined.

We grabbed some treats and jumped in the car to give pursuit, but the dog had disappeared. We drove up the road one way and then came back another. We strained to see into the woods. Nothing.

Betsy began to cry. "We rescued him only to lose him again. He's worse off than ever now."

We circled around our country block again, about four miles or so, calling and scanning the woods and the road. We simply did not see him.

Betsy said, "I think we need to go home and call the shelter. Maybe he is headed back there."

But neither of us believed it. Our new dog was gone. He was in new territory, had on a harness that belonged to someone else and could put him at risk of getting caught in brush, and had no name that we knew. We had no idea what we should do. If we'd had some bread with us, we might have caught him quickly, but we didn't know that yet.

Dejected, we returned home. I cannot even begin to explain how devastated and worried we felt. And then the miracle happened. We looked out into the dog fence and—was it possible?—one … two … three … Wait! there were four beautiful faces looking back at us. The new dog had come home on his own and was hanging with his new dog mates. We never did learn how he got back into the enclosure, but surely he'd been zapped by the electric fence as he climbed in to join the others. We never knew how he knew this was his new home. We never figured out why he came back, but he did. We opened the fence. All four trooped in like that was the way it had always been.

"What shall we name him?" I asked.

Betsy looked up and smiled. In a moment of what seemed unusual clarity when it came to dog naming, she said, "I think we should name him Ichabod, after Ichabod Crane. He has the gangly legs, the big nose …"

She trailed off as she saw my face. I thought the name was, well, kind of dumb. She continued to explain that we had a kind of theme going. We had a dog named Spirit, which is ghostlike, I guess. So Ichabod fit. In a last-ditch effort, I said,

"Well, you have to promise not to call him 'Icky.'" We did, of course. But most of the time, this sweet dog, who seemed to have chosen our home when he had the opportunity to run free, went by Ichabod.

Gary, Bayley, and Ichabod

Chapter 11

Really? Another Dog?

But we still worried about Bayley. While he did his best to keep up with a much taller, much stronger Ichabod, we felt it was not a good long-term match. We already had four dogs, something a few years ago we couldn't have imagined, so should we consider getting another skijoring dog? Would five dogs be that much different than four? And to be honest, we rather enjoyed our group of dogs and our newfound sport.

We talked, and we dreamed, and we thought. We really loved the Border Collie mentality that Bayley had shown us, his quickness in training, basic trust when he was off leash, his incredible focus when he knew what job he was to do. After the last horrific experiences when he escaped, Bayley never again left our yard. Maybe what we needed to run alongside Ichabod was another healthier, stronger, bigger Border Collie.

Our daughter, who had moved to Cape Cod with her two Border Collies, had developed a bit of a relationship with the Border Collie community there. Amy had a friend who had a friend whose Border Collie was expecting. We suddenly were filled with excitement about adding a new puppy to our crew of dogs. The timing was right—it was spring, and somehow it felt like this was the right thing to do. We called the owners of the pregnant dog and asked a number of questions. We were surprised to find out that his Border Collies, while primarily trained to herd sheep, were also trained to pull a sled in winter to keep them busy and in shape. It sounded like the perfect combination of breed and experience.

We gulped a bit at the price—$500, the most we had ever spent on a dog—but we asked that he save us the largest male puppy from the litter and sent in our deposit. More quickly than usual, now that we had a theme going for dog names, we chose the name Casper, after the friendly ghost. It was a new record, since Casper was not even born yet. We asked the owner to begin calling him his name as soon as he was born.

We then settled down to wait for the birth and some pictures of our new puppy. He arrived, and he was beautiful in the pictures they sent. We were definitely falling in love

Betsy and Casper

164

already. Since we lived many hours from the breeder, we were not able to visit until the day arrived to take him home.

We hired a dog sitter to take care of Spirit, Neeka, and Ichabod, loaded Bayley in the car, and headed off to Cape Cod to bring Casper home.

We arrived at the breeder's house and finally saw real, live Casper for the first time. We were a bit shocked. We looked at each other, barely believing our eyes. Casper was tiny, tiny, tiny. I am not sure where the discussions about selecting the biggest dog of the litter went, but Casper was definitely not it. He was tiny and very delicate-looking. And cute! And we had already fallen in love with him, so he was ours, regardless of his size.

We brought Bayley in, and the breeder was surprised to see his unusual tri-coloring, calling him a clown-colored Border Collie, whatever that meant. Bayley was polite but reserved when he was introduced to Casper, and that remained their relationship for their whole lives together. Casper absolutely adored Bayley, who would move politely away when Casper came to cuddle with him. Bayley's best friend was clearly Spirit, and the two often slept side by side, or with one of their heads resting upon the other.

As we often did when we traveled to Cape Cod, we went to Provincetown just to walk around and see the sights. We had Bayley and Casper along with us and, of course, the tiny puppy drew quite a bit of attention. I know the man who made the comment did not mean to insult our tiny dog when he saw little Casper resting in Betsy's arms, with his feet crossed delicately across her hands, when he said, "What a sweet little dog, and so clearly a female."

Some dogs seem to adjust to riding in a car with nary a problem. Unfortunately, this was not Casper. The ride back to New York was long, indeed. Casper cried and threw up on Betsy most of the seven hours it took to get home. We would stop and clean up both Betsy and Casper, and then continue toward home. Betsy finally discovered that Casper seemed more comfortable, and would not cry or throw up, when he was held gently under his front legs and was swung slowly back and forth, back and forth. Finally, Betsy and Casper fell into an exhausted sleep, and Bayley seemed to be saying, "I could have warned you about this dog."

PART 2

BETSY

Introduction to Part 2

S hortly after we brought Casper home, Gary, who was *never* a complainer, mentioned he had been feeling tired and was fighting to find energy to complete even the simplest of tasks. We thought that perhaps he had some sort of virus and, after a brief checkup with his doctor, decided to make a planned trip to help our daughter and her family move into their new home in The Woodlands, Texas. It was a beautiful place, and although certainly urban, filled with ponds and walkways and lots of trees. We were excited for them and eager to help. We also always loved an excuse to see our little granddaughter.

Something, though, was clearly wrong with Gary. He would start the day feeling generally okay, but by afternoon was running a high fever, couldn't eat, spiked astronomically high blood sugar levels, and would have to go to bed. Since he was a diabetic, the fevers, high blood sugar levels, and lack of consistent eating were concerning to us and, by the third day of this cycle, we went to the emergency room at The Woodlands' hospital. They ran blood work, asked if he had traveled out of the country, and noted that his white blood cells were high, along with other abnormalities, suggesting that perhaps he had picked up some kind of parasite. No one prepared us for what was to come.

We were extremely eager to get back home, and somehow felt that just getting home would be what Gary needed to recover. As we boarded the plane, I was shocked to see my strong, active husband struggling to handle the incline to the plane's door. He had to stop several times and was clearly very ill. We arrived home and planned to go to the doctor's the next day. But as we got to our driveway, I knew that we couldn't wait until morning. I turned our car around and drove the forty-five minutes back to Syracuse, where we had just left.

I don't know if anyone is ever ready to hear devastating health news, but we surely were not. After several tests, including a painful bone marrow test, the doctor sat down next to Gary's bed and informed us that Gary had AML, Acute Myeloid Leukemia. I rushed to the head of Gary's bed and gently held him as we both digested this news. He was fifty-two years old. It was May 1999.

All kinds of thoughts were roiling through my head. *What if he doesn't want to fight this? Will we ever again eat together on our deck on a sunny summer day? Is this a clear death sentence? What are the treatments? What about the dogs? Will I be able to keep them and care for them by myself?* And, finally, *how do I tell our children?* This last question, how to tell our adult children, seemed almost insurmountable at first. I felt sick to my stomach at the thought.

The doctor explained that the treatment is pretty barbaric and would require weeks-long hospitalization. He also shared his frustration at how much doctors do not know about this illness. I appreciated his honesty and his trust in us to handle it. I managed to tell our children, keeping my message hopeful. We were able to eat again on our deck on a sunny summer day, when Gary would get a short reprieve from his hospital stays. I kept and rejoiced in our dogs. Yes, as it turned out, it *was* a death sentence, and the treatments *were* barbaric. But my husband chose to fight. His courage in the face of this horrific disease was inspiring to us all. He lived for a year, endured two bone marrow transplants, and was upbeat and hopeful to the end.

But Gary always wanted this book to be about the dogs—and the two people who had always thought that more than one dog was just, well, wrong. I am not exactly sure why the prospect of having multiple dogs had been a problem for us, but it was. I would watch others who had several dogs and wonder about the people. Somehow it just seemed that having more than one dog would reduce the quality of life of the dogs *and* the people. Or, perhaps, we felt that having multiple dogs suggested the owners didn't have very full lives beyond their dogs. In any case, we had been quite clear with each other that, while we could not imagine a life without a dog, we were definitely a one-dog family.

We had strayed from that on two previous occasions, when our children raised two dogs for Guiding Eyes through a 4-H program. Our first experience was with a sweet, little black Labrador named Elizabeth. She lived with us for a year, and ultimately became a guiding eye dog for a blind woman who helped the newly blind cope with their blindness. Arriving at the Guiding Eyes facility to watch Elizabeth and her new partner was amazing, heartwarming, and a little sad. We were allowed to greet Elizabeth after the graduation ceremony. She was almost overcome with joy at seeing us again, and our hearts broke a bit as we left her behind. The parting was eased a bit as the woman that became Elizabeth's partner often sent us letters and pictures of Elizabeth and their many adventures.

Our second guiding eye dog, a beautiful Golden Retriever named Charlie, also stayed with us a year, but after several months of training at the guiding eye training center, was proclaimed just "too much dog," and we were invited to reclaim him. When I think of it now, I don't know exactly why we thought we could not comfortably take Charlie back, but we were still certain that we were a one-dog family. A friend, however, very much wanted Charlie, so the dog returned to our hometown with a new family. Other than those two occasions, we were seldom without a dog, but always just one. Now we had five dogs and couldn't imagine our life any other way. We had changed.

Chapter 12

A Surprise Sixth Dog

It's hard to imagine now, but as Gary was finishing up a rough and lengthy second round of chemotherapy, our friend Laurie called. She was crying, and asked, "Please, would you consider taking Sierra?"

Sierra was her eleven-month-old Border Collie. This was the woman who had taken such good care of Bayley shortly after his pins were removed, and who had enjoyed pet-sitting for him on several occasions after that. She was so taken with Bayley's laid-back and loving personality that she had gotten her own Border Collie, not quite recognizing that our laid-back Border did not represent all Borders and most are not particularly designed for city apartment living, where they are asked to spend eight to twelve hours a day in a crate.

"Sierra is destructive," Laurie explained.

Who wouldn't be? I thought.

"She chews up everything, digs holes in my yard, and doesn't do anything I say."

Of course, anyone who has had a puppy, especially one that needs stimulation and a job to do, knows that these are just puppy things.

But Laurie was distraught and begging us to take her puppy. It appeared that Laurie truly loved her dog, but that the environment was not the right one for her active Border Collie. We also thought there might have been a little pressure being placed on our friend by her boyfriend, who admitted he had hit the dog on some occasions, trying to train her.

The call had come when Gary had just gone into remission. With the uncertainty as to the course of his disease, it seemed logical that we should say no. We talked it over.

"Yes," we said. "We will take her."

Sierra was a beautiful, classically marked Border Collie. Her owner brought her up to us, and we watched as she greeted our other dogs. Things went well. Now, rather unexpectedly, we were the owners of six dogs.

About three weeks later, we got another call from Laurie. She was crying, "I think about Sierra every day, and I really want her back. Please understand. I'm so sorry."

So off went Sierra, back with her original owner. Two more weeks went by, and we got a call again. "I just can't handle Sierra. Please, can I bring her back?"

We hesitated. We didn't want to play this back-and-forth game with this poor dog's life. "Yes," we said, "but we will not return her again."

While Gary was briefly in remission, we began to train our dogs for skijoring in earnest. We were optimistic that Gary would beat leukemia and looked forward to racing over the winter. It was then the middle of fall, and the weather was perfect for training. Gary was not strong enough to take them out on his bike, but I was, and I enjoyed Gary slowly driving behind us in the car, as I took the dogs out in twos and threes, pulling me on my bike.

Sierra, it turned out, loved to run and to pull. While she was a bit bossy with the other dogs, particularly the Huskies, she was totally focused whenever we got out her harness and hooked her up with another dog. She was fast and quick to train, and she ran with great joy. Sometimes Sierra ran as Casper's partner, two Border Collies running with smiles on their faces. Sometimes Sierra ran with a Husky, a wonderful combination of Husky power and Border Collie speed, along with serious dedication to her job. We could have never imagined it a few years before, but now we were a six-dog family and these dogs filled our hearts, helping keep us in the present as Gary and I faced the fear and uncertainty his illness placed on our future.

Sierra

Chapter 13

We Need to Keep Training

In spite of Gary's illness, we decided I needed to continue to train the dogs that first fall. For brief periods, Gary was allowed home, and would follow us in our car, where he could be a part of the action in some limited way. When he was in the hospital, which was most of the time, I would train them alone. Since we had six dogs, this usually meant going out with them pulling my bike three times, with a different two-dog team each time. I typically started with the fastest team, Casper and Ichabod; then take the second-fastest team, Neeka and Sierra; and, finally, the slowest team, Spirit and Bayley. While taking my handmade rig was generally a safer way to go, it was rather unstable, and was hard for me to get on the car, so I usually trained them using my bicycle when we didn't have snow.

One day, in late fall, I loaded up the dogs and bike and headed for the trails up east. I hooked up Casper and Ichabod to the tug line and attached the tug line to my bike. They ran steady and fast, and we had a quick two-mile run. I returned for Neeka and Sierra and, again, they were slightly slower, but ran steadily.

Finally, I hooked up Spirit and Bayley and we headed out. We were moving fairly well when something in the woods caught Spirit's attention. In the split second that she glanced off to the left for a better view, she slightly slowed her pace. The change in speed surprised me, and I was not able to compensate quickly enough to avoid running up on the tug line. It caught the wheel, brought my bike to an abrupt stop, and the next thing I knew, I was flying over the handlebars. I was airborne long enough to have a clear thought—*This is really going to hurt.*

I fell hard on my left shoulder and wrist, and the handlebars embedded themselves into my thigh. The dogs stopped almost instantly. Thankfully, the tug line has a bungee-like section that helps soften the impact on the dogs in the event of a quick change in speed or an abrupt stop like this. They seemed okay, but I was hurting. Slowly and carefully, I stood up. Almost everything hurt, but I needed to get back to the car. I untangled the tug line and climbed back on my bike. We all slowly made our way back to the car.

By the next day, my wrist and shoulder had swollen up, and I had a hematoma on my thigh that was about five to seven inches in diameter. I was afraid I might have broken my wrist or my shoulder, so made a visit to my doctor, who, after doing X-rays, was surprised there was no fracture. I was relieved. It was not until later that we discovered that I had torn my rotator cuff, and it caused me problems for months. It didn't stop me from training my dogs, though, and my hematoma impressed people for weeks.

After my spectacular fall, I was apprehensive about training the dogs on my bike. The rig my father had made was not stable enough for running over dirt roads, particularly given the power of a two- or three-dog team. We needed a mushing rig. Gary and I checked online, where catalog prices for rigs ranged from $500 to $1,000. This price tag was simply

Betsy, Spirit, and Neeka bike training

too much for us. We wondered if we might be able to find a used one that was more affordable. We called a mushing friend to see if he knew of any secondhand rigs that might be for sale. We found one for $200. This was still more than we wanted to spend. We called another musher, and he had one he indicated was in generally good shape but had worn brakes. It was $50.

"Perfect," we said. "We will take it."

The owner suggested that we add a hitch to the back of our car, so we could pull it to our training sites. We bought the rig and called my dad, who always seemed up for a welding job.

Pulling the rig slowly on the back of our car worked well. Now we had to find out if the rig would work with our dogs, or if they would be confused or frightened by pulling something totally different behind them. I hooked up Ichabod, Casper, and Sierra. They took off at great speed, not ever seeming to notice that I was following behind in a rather large, rather noisy rig. Gary followed carefully behind in our car. It was muddy, and I was getting covered with mud, but I was having fun and felt much safer nearer the ground.

That is until I started down a small hill and went to put on the brakes. Nothing. I tried again. Nothing. I had forgotten that the previous owner had warned us the brakes were worn. I was gaining speed on the dogs and desperately trying not to overrun them. I dropped one foot to the road and dragged it for all I was worth. It slowed the rig enough that I did not hit any dogs, but I knew we would need to fix the brakes as soon as possible. I also knew that the rig was going to work.

Sometime after Gary's death, I realized that I wanted to find something that was smaller, lighter, and easier to move than the rig. I discovered a dog scooter, made in Australia. I thought, *This would be perfect for training my dogs on dirt roads.*

The wheels were quite large, it had good brakes, and was lightweight. I saved money for a few months and then ordered my scooter. Since it came from Australia, I had to wait several more weeks, but finally it arrived. It had hand brakes and a roomy place for me to stand. It was almost like a cross between a bike and a rig. Since my fall, I really liked to be nearer the ground when I trained, so this was just what I wanted.

A friend, Heather, who did some skijoring, was impressed with my scooter and sent for one as well. One fall day, Heather and I on our scooters, and her boyfriend on a bicycle, decided to do some training together. The dogs were always excited to see other teams and were eager to go. My dogs charged off. I was smiling as we moved quickly along the wooded road, enjoying the beauty of the brightly colored fall trees. Roy started a few minutes after me on a bike, but quickly caught up, as he had very strong dogs, and could help them along by pedaling.

Heather, though, got off to a rather slow start, as her dogs seemed less interested in a run and she had a few issues as she was hooking them up. Roy and I were headed back toward our cars when I saw Heather heading toward us. As if in slow motion, I watched as Roy's dogs, in their attempt to move over, went the wrong way and ended up stretching their tug line across the road directly in the path of Heather, who at this point was moving along quite nicely. My mouth opened to give a shout of warning, but it was too late. Heather's dogs ran under the tug line, but Heather and her scooter ran directly into it.

She flew from the scooter, landing in a water- and leaf-filled ditch, face first. It was really a spectacular and quite beautiful fall. Roy was muttering under his breath as he untangled his dogs from Heather's dogs and trying to find a way to blame Heather for the mishap. I ran to Heather. She lifted her face slowly from the muddy ditch, spitting out pieces of leaves, water, and mud.

"That was a rather soft landing," she said.

Sometime later, my daughter Shelley and her two children, Christopher and Lauren, were visiting from Texas. A friend and her daughter, another Lauren, asked if they might have a ride with me on the scooter with the dogs pulling. It seemed safe enough, even though the children were two, four, and five years old. My dogs were gentle and generally easily controlled. We made the short trip to Wart Road on Tug Hill. I hooked up two dogs, loaded four-year-old Lauren, my friend's daughter, onto the scooter, and off we went. The dogs ran about half a mile out and then back, making for a fun one-mile run.

The road was straight, so Shelley and her kids and Lauren's mother could watch as we moved cleanly and swiftly along.

We returned safely, and both my grandchildren were eager to try. Since Chris was only two, I felt I should take the slowest dogs and go a fairly short distance. Again, the dogs ran steadily, and both observers and participants were having a great time.

Finally, it was my five-year-old granddaughter Lauren's turn. She was excited and eagerly climbed onto the scooter with me. As I had with each of the other children, I reminded her to hang on tightly to the handlebars and not let go, no matter what. I had hooked up Neeka and Bayley this time, to give them a chance to run, and off we went. We were about a half mile down the road when something caught Neeka's attention.

It is amazing how little it takes, in terms of a change in stride, to cause a catastrophic outcome. The small jerk was enough to throw both Lauren and me from the scooter. I could feel what was coming and feared I was going to fall right on top of Lauren. In a last-ditch effort to avoid that, I kicked firmly off the back of the scooter, and we went flying. My kick propelled me off to the side of Lauren rather than on top of her, but it also increased our falling momentum. We both lay stunned on the road.

The dogs stopped and turned around to see what had happened. Lauren was eerily quiet at first, and then her screams started. I quickly picked her up, fearing broken bones. Thankfully, all of her bones were intact, but she had one of the worst road burns I had ever seen. The whole left side of her face was pocked and bleeding, with small pieces of gravel embedded deeply into her skin. Her left arm and leg were similarly injured.

Lauren, Ichabod, and Chris

I held her as her cries quieted, and she looked me directly in the face and said, "I'm so sorry, Grandma. I let go of the handlebars."

I nearly cried as she spoke and assured her that the jerk of the scooter made it impossible for anyone to hold on. I told her how sorry I was that she had been hurt. Then, I looked at her, bleeding and covered in gravel, and said, "I'm sorry, Lauren, but we need to get back on the scooter so we can get back to your mom."

She gamely climbed on, and we successfully made it back to her mom, brother, and our friends.

When we got home, we carefully cleaned her wounds and put antibiotic ointment on them. Her mom and I talked. Shelley's husband, who had not accompanied his family on this trip, was always very nervous about letting his children take risks, and was fairly certain I was crazy when I allowed them to walk along our shallow pond, even with supervision; climb along a stone fence; or any number of other things I felt were good for developing confidence and for just plain having fun. Taking his children for a ride behind dogs on a scooter was likely way beyond anything even close to his comfort level. Shelley and her children were returning to Houston the day after Lauren's fall, and the wounds were likely to look even worse than they did now—and they were definitely bad. Shelley thought that in the best interest of everyone, she would simply say that Lauren had taken a bad fall, leaving out the part about riding with her grandma behind dogs. That was okay with me, since I was already on his questionable list.

We arrived at the airline counter the next day, where Shelley and her children were getting their tickets. The check-in staff person looked over the counter at Lauren and said, "Oh honey, how did you get hurt?"

All thoughts about lying or giving the partial truth, flew out the window as Lauren said, "I was riding on a scooter with Grandma and the dogs were pulling us. We fell off. The dogs didn't mean to hurt me, and they said 'sorry.' I said sorry, too, because I forgot to hang on."

We forgot about the fact that Lauren had experienced this and could, in fact, talk.

It is with great joy that this same Lauren, who is now a full-fledged adult, agreed to do the cover drawing for this book, bringing this book into the next generation of Water-man's.

❄ ❄ ❄

Sometime after my impressive fall from the bike, and before Lauren's, Heather and I decided to sneak three of the dogs into the hospital to visit Gary. Our plan was to walk confidently into the hospital like we belonged there, climb on the elevator, and make our way to the oncology floor. Some people gave us some interesting looks, but they seemed to be saying, "They must have permission, or they certainly wouldn't be leading these dogs right down the hallways of the hospital."

Gary's face lit up as the dogs entered his private room. Casper and Bayley immediately jumped up on his bed and laid down. We held our breath as a nurse came into the room, acted a bit surprised, but immediately went about her business taking Gary's blood pressure and other vitals, smiled at us, and left the room. Soon other nurses and a doctor arrived at the room and again, things stood still for a moment, until one of the nurses said, "My what beautiful dogs. It must be great for you to see them." No one hollered. No one kicked us out.

A few more minutes passed, Gary enjoying the closeness of the dogs he loved so much, and my friend and I were thankful we had been able to connect Gary with some of his dogs, when a nurse came into the room and quietly touched my sleeve.

"I wondered if you might bring the dogs in to see Mary. She is in the room at the end of the hall. She has been very sad and seldom has visitors, and I think a visit from your dogs might help her."

"Of course," we said, leaving two of the dogs with Gary and bringing Bayley to visit with Mary, as we did not want to overwhelm her.

Bayley, whose whole being had always been filled with love, climbed up onto Mary's bed as if he knew just what to do, and gently laid his head on her stomach. Mary nuzzled her face into Bayley's fur and silently cried. I still cry when I think of that moment. We later learned that Mary was nearing the end of her fight with cancer, and that she had requested her husband, children, and friends not see her in her rapidly deteriorating condition. I grieved for them all, as I would later see her husband sitting outside her room, keeping vigil, honoring her request. I was glad that Gary wanted me there and that we were able to make the tough journey together.

In early November, 1999, Gary finally went into a remission and was released from the hospital. We are both optimistic by nature and were pretty sure he had beaten this rotten disease. We were both filled with joy as we came home and Gary could see his dogs again. The dogs crowded around Gary, giving him kisses and leaning their bodies into him. We didn't realize it at first, but the enthusiasm of the other dogs was leaving Ichabod pushed to the side.

He made his presence known, however, when he jumped up onto the dining room table, to get a better vantage point and to let us know he was there. Perhaps it wouldn't have been so startling if he had been a smaller dog, but Ichabod was *not* small and was, in fact, very tall and gangly. He not only jumped onto the table, but he also raised up for a moment or two on his hind feet, giving himself even more of a presence. We definitely noticed! We reminded him that dogs don't belong on the table, and he reminded us that he wanted his share of the attention. Mostly, we just laughed.

The next day we were all still enjoying being together, and all of us, including the dogs, were excited. Just how excited was demonstrated in something our dogs rarely did—pee in the wrong places. I had gone out to pick up a small statue in my flower garden, and it crumbled to pieces in my hand. I was grumbling about that just as I backed up and stepped into dog poop.

Okay, I thought. *It is still a good day. It is still a good day. No problem.*

Sierra, perhaps noticing my mild distress, chose that moment to jump up on me and give me one of her hugs around the neck. I lifted her off the ground in my arms, with her rear feet dangling, as I often did when she hugged me. Then I felt something warm running down my leg.

Okay. I can clean myself up, I thought, *and Sierra and I had a bonding moment.* I got myself cleaned up, and we had the dogs mostly settled in our bedroom for the night. I went to climb into bed and again felt something warm and wet on my side of the bed. Casper had just peed on the bed, something he had literally *never* done before. I think it spoke volumes about the emotions we were all feeling.

Shortly after Gary was discharged from the hospital, he decided he wanted to try our new, used rig. He hooked up Ichabod, Spirit, Casper, and Bayley. Bayley started hanging back right away, unable to keep up with the others. As Gary was trying to find the brake on the rig to slow the rest of the team down, he lost his footing and rolled the rig. The dogs stopped and stood still. I was following him in the car and quickly pulled to the side of the dirt road.

"Are you okay?" I shouted.

"Just a little bumped up," he said, rolling the rig back onto its wheels and climbing back on.

But he was hurt. His leg swelled badly, and his doctor gave him a stern lecture about taking unnecessary risks.

"But it was fun," answered Gary. "It was fun."

Sadly, by Thanksgiving, it was clear the leukemia was back, and the only hope was for Gary to have a bone marrow transplant, something that would require his treatment to continue in Rochester, about two hours from our home. We were disappointed, a bit angry, sad, and afraid. I decided to take a leave of absence from my teaching job so I could stay at the hospital for longer periods. That also meant that we needed to make other arrangements for our dogs. While he was in Syracuse, I would typically make the trip back home each night from the hospital, and when I did stay with him overnight, one of our older granddaughters would stay and take care of the dogs.

That was going to be considerably harder to do now that the traveling distance was more than twice as far. We talked about possible solutions and decided that we needed to find temporary homes for our dogs. This nearly broke our hearts, but we knew that we could not ask a person to stay at our house for extended periods, or for a single family to take on the added burden of all six dogs. We decided we needed to split them up.

A mushing friend took Ichabod to his house with his dogs. Spirit and Bayley, who were very anxious when sepa-rated, went together to stay with my father. Casper went to stay with our son's friend Charles. Neeka went to stay with my niece, Kristen, and her red Husky, who looked amazingly like Neeka. Sierra stayed with our son, Jeremy. We knew they were all safe, but we had become a team, and parting with them, even temporarily, was very painful. But we did what we had to do.

Gary's treatment became even more complicated when an initial search for a bone marrow transplant donor among his siblings suggested there were no matches, meaning they might have to search the national donor list to find a possible match. We had researched all this a bit and discovered that the best place for unrelated bone marrow transplants, at least at the time, was at a well-known hospital in the state of Washington. We contacted the hospital, which wanted to run its own blood tests on Gary's brothers and sisters to see if the original findings were accurate. They were not. Our hearts soared as we learned both of Gary's brothers were good matches, and the best match was with the brother who lived nearby. The problem now was that they needed to get Gary into remission again before they could do the transplant. As was the case the first time, the disease was stubborn, and took months of hospitalization until they found no diseased cells in his marrow, essentially because they had destroyed nearly all of it.

They did the transplant, and Gary was very sick for several weeks. Then it looked like it had worked. He was in remission again and out of the hospital by May. We brought all our dogs home and were a family again. We took a trip to Texas to see a new grandson who was only a few months old, and his sister, whom we had not seen for months. We thought, once again, that Gary had beaten this horrible disease.

But again, remission did not last more than a few weeks. The dogs were welcomed back into the homes where they had stayed for several months before, and once more, Gary and I went back to take on leukemia. The doctors recognized Gary's commitment to life and worked to find a cure that would work. They were amazed by Gary's spirit and determination. He seldom complained.

One day, as we were riding in the car back to Rochester, I asked him, "Are you afraid to die? Does it frighten you?" I still smile at his answer.

"I am not afraid to die. I just don't intend to."

Chapter 14

Gary's Death

Gary's determination and courage were recognized by all who treated him. Gary's primary oncologist told us that when Gary said something like, "I need to ask you a question," the doctor would hold his breath for what would come next. He said he was used to patients asking, "Can I take a short ride and get some ice cream?" But Gary's questions were more like "Can I take a hike in the Adirondacks while I am home?" "Can I go canoe camping?" "Can I run the dogs?"

It was this determination that made his doctor decide to try a second bone marrow transplant, even though it was highly unlikely to work, and they could not wait until he was in remission to try it. The doctor said, "Gary has beaten the odds over and over again. I don't want to give up yet."

But within days of the second transplant, his lungs filled with dead and dying cells, and he was placed on a breathing machine until it was clear his organs were all failing. His children and small grandchildren; his brother, who had given his cells for two transplants, and my sister-in-law; several close friends; a minister from his childhood; and I gathered around his bed to stay with him as they removed the breathing tube. We all began to sing the Doxology, because it was a song we all knew, and, quietly, Gary died.

Our daughter who had flown in from Texas had brought her two very young children to be with us. I remember them sitting calmly on their grandfather's bed as he slipped into the next world. Eerily, they both cried out at the moment Gary's spirit left this earth, and then were quiet and peaceful. It was July 20, 2000, the day after my birthday.

Gary's memorial service was a happy affair. He had been a conductor of a large local community choral group for several years before he died. We had also both been members of our church's choir. The community chorus, complete with banjo backup, sang Kermit the Frog's "Rainbow Connection" and "Somewhere Out There," and an expanded church choir sang one of my favorite moving spirituals, "The Majesty and Glory of His Name."

Several people from different areas of Gary's varied and active life spoke about him. One particularly moving moment was when a good friend asked him to let us all know if there was skiing in heaven. I surprised many people at the service because, in an effort to involve as many people as possible in the memorial service, I gave several people pieces of paper with quotations that were meaningful to Gary and me. One after another, they stood, quietly reading each quote, in turn. As the readings came to a close all the readers stood together and, to honor Gary's love for Star Wars, as one they read one last quote: "May the force be with you."

And with that, the celebrants of Gary's life went to enjoy a beautiful meal together.

Chapter 15

Camping

Immediately after Gary's death, I brought all my dogs home and tried to explain to them that Gary was gone. They seemed to understand. The comfort that my six crazy dogs and one rescued Persian cat provided me cannot be overstated. I had little time to feel sorry for myself as I dived back into work and concentrated on giving the dogs the attention and exercise they needed each day.

My friend Heather and I often took the dogs for swims at a reservoir a few miles from my home. I could not help but smile at them romping in the water in their own special way. On such adventures, Sierra was busy, and did not act aggressively toward the others, so these jaunts were peaceful and fun for both dogs and humans.

Before Gary got sick, we went on many canoe camping trips, often paddling and carrying our canoe deep into Algonquin Park in Ontario, Canada. We got started canoe camping, however, a bit hesitantly. As a family with young children, we often went camping with friends and their children at various campgrounds. The kids had a wonderful time on these outings, as they had friends to play with, and the campgrounds almost always had game rooms and pools to enjoy. I, however, often felt like these camping adventures primarily required days of packing and days of unpacking. I did have fun sitting around the campfire in the evening with friends, but the work involved in these trips was always a little overwhelming, and sometimes seemed to take longer than the actual camping stays.

One time, we arrived rather late at a campground in Pennsylvania and hurried to get the tent set up and dinner fixed. As we were just about to finish setting up the tent, we discovered that a key piece—the part that essentially held the tent together at the top of the whole affair—was missing. After a little hissing at each other for not checking to make sure the tent parts were all there, we were able to duct-tape it together well enough to sleep in.

After three or four days, it was time to pack up our things and head for home. Gary and I were left totally speechless as we rolled up the tent and realized the part had been laying on the ground, under the tent floor, the whole time. That annoying tree root we thought we had been sleeping on was the missing, critical part.

I would like to say that these kinds of mishaps were infrequent, but that would not be true. Camping nearly always became a challenge. While the romantic parts of us loved the idea, the work of transporting enough gear for five people, sometimes more when our children's friends joined us, was often daunting. One day, Gary and I looked at each other and said, almost collectively, "I think we should just stay in motels from now on." And that had remained the crux of our camping plans until our kids were grown. And eventually they *were* grown.

"I would really like to try some primitive canoe camping," I said one day, perhaps a bit out of the blue, after having read about someone else's exciting adventure.

Gary answered, "I thought we were staying in motels for the rest of our lives. That still seems like a good idea to me."

I persisted. "But things are different now that our kids are on their own. The packing should be much less difficult for just the two of us."

"But we know nothing about canoeing. We don't even *own* a canoe," Gary countered.

He wasn't wrong, but I was determined. I bought a book about canoe camping. I would read a passage or two to him from time to time, but he still was very skeptical about the whole idea.

Ultimately, we compromised. We would try a canoe camping trip but would take enough money to finish our vacation in a motel if either one of us was not having fun. We decided on a trip to the Adirondack Mountains, about an hour and a half from our home. We borrowed most of the gear we needed from a friend, rented a canoe, and, carrying and dragging our stuff, we walked about a mile back into the area around Nelson Lake for a four-day stay. Except for one brief thunderstorm, the weather was glorious, and the storm added a little extra excitement.

Gary paddled around and fished while I lay in the back of the canoe and read. We picked wild blueberries and made shortcakes with a mix I had brought and an oven we made over an open fire out of aluminum foil. In fact, it was while the shortcakes were baking that the thunderstorm moved in, drenching our fire and the little oven. But the shortcakes still were mostly cooked and tasted better than anything I had ever had. We laid in the sun and took little day hikes. At the end of our four days, we had both fallen in love with canoeing and camping. This kind of camping was significantly different than the kind of camping we had done in the past. This was not a busy, noisy campground. We had the only campsite on a beautiful lake.

At the end of our trip, we returned the rented canoe and the borrowed gear and began our search for our own canoe. We knew we wanted one made of Kevlar, as we planned to be making long carries at times, but new ones were clearly out of our price range. We asked friends, we checked *The Swap Sheet*, and we stumbled upon a whitewater, down river, Mad River racing canoe. The gunnels were broken and partially missing, there were no seats, and there were scratches and small dented areas all around the canoe's body. Racing it down fast-moving rivers and banging it into rocks had taken its toll. But it was $300, and we thought it was beautiful.

It was fall, and the weather was a bit cool, but we bought the canoe and some paddles, strapped the canoe to our car, and off we went to a local stream to try it out. We kneeled in the canoe, since it had no seats, steadied ourselves, and were off, down the stream. Since it was a racing canoe, the bottom was very curved. Any movement caused the canoe to rock, which was a little scary, but soon we learned that, in spite of the sensitivity to movement, it was stable, it floated, and best of all, it was ours!

That winter we spent much of our free time researching and reading about the best gear for primitive canoe camping. We also had heard from a friend about Algonquin Provincial Park in Ontario and bought a map of the park and water trails. It was exciting to dream together of our next summer's adventure, something we did each winter for the next ten years.

The spring following the purchase of our canoe, we bought seats and new gunnels for it. Some friends needed to replace the gunnels on their canoe, so we had a gunnel replacement party. This was great for us, because they were experienced canoers and had done other canoe repairs. It took a few days, but in the end, the new gunnels looked magnificent.

"I think we need to paint our canoe," I said. "It would look so great if you didn't see all of the patch jobs. I would like to paint it yellow."

"Paint will just add weight," Gary said, rather logically. "And we got a Kevlar canoe so it would be as light as possible."

"But I really want it to look pretty," I persisted. And privately, I thought, *How much weight can paint really add?*

So off we went to a marine store and bought some bright yellow paint. Over the years, though, I realized that Gary was right. You just don't paint a Kevlar canoe. But I was naïve and had a bit of a romantic image about what our first canoe should look like. My confidence in my decision to add paint, though, was dashed a bit every time a person saw our canoe and, rather incredulously, asked, "But why would you paint a Kevlar canoe?" Why, indeed.

That first summer after we got our *new* canoe, we made our first trip to Algonquin Provincial Park. We planned to travel some of the backcountry routes, which required a number of carries. We were still learning about how important lightweight gear was. Our plan was to take two trips at each carry. Gary would use the yoke we had added to the middle of the canoe to carry it over his head. I would carry a large backpack containing most of our gear. We would return for a second dry sack of food and miscellaneous items we hadn't really learned how to pack yet.

We were quite happy with this system until about the fourth day of our six-day trip. We spotted an older couple who appeared to be going the same direction as us. We knew that around supper time we would be arriving at a lake that had only one campsite. We assumed they were heading for the same lake and, because they were ahead of us, it looked like they would get to the site first. We really wanted that campsite and would certainly be willing to share the site with them, but we wanted to be the ones inviting them, not the ones being invited.

Gary and I looked at each other. Competitiveness reared its ugly head.

"If we can cross the next three carries in one trip, we should be able to beat them to the lake," Gary said. The food bag had gotten lighter over the course of the trip, and Gary was certain he could carry the canoe, paddles, and food bag in one trip.

"If I tie our water bucket unto the dry sack, and carry the other extra things in my hands, I think I can make it in one trip, too." I said.

We started to hurry. The other couple had been beginning their second carry across, just as we were arriving for our first trip across, each time we saw them.

The race to the site was on. We were definitely catching them, and they appeared to have sped up their trips across—running, carrying their gear in bare feet.

We arrived at the crossing to our last lake of the day at about the same time, but they still had two trips to make while we were doing it in one. We had done it. We had beaten these two people, who were at least twenty years older than us and running across rugged terrain in bare feet, to the campsite.

"Would you like to share the site with us tonight?" we generously asked as they paddled up the lake.

"No, thanks," they replied. "We plan to do at least a couple more lakes before stopping for the night."

Did I mention they were doing the carries in bare feet?

❄ ❄ ❄

I was perfectly happy with our paddling skills, and we made rather efficient canoers, I thought. But as was Gary's style, once he was invested in a sport, he wanted to become better and better. He would regularly bring advertisements to me for paddling camps.

"I really want to go to this paddling camp in Maine this summer," Gary would say.

"Sounds good," I would say, secretly hoping he would forget the whole thing. I enjoy just *doing* stuff, not necessarily practicing for it. Gary always wanted to learn how to do it better, more efficiently, faster, longer. I just wanted to do it.

❄ ❄ ❄

After Gary died, I feared I would never go canoe camping again. I hated the idea that I would always have to ask someone to go with me and hated even more that they would say yes because they felt sorry for me. Up until this point, I hadn't done any solo canoeing or kayaking. Gary was always my partner, and although we never did make it to a paddle training camp, we had become very efficient paddlers—always paddling in sync, strokes together, with Gary calling out "switch" when it was time to stroke on the other side. When we were traveling some distance in a day, we had a stroke/ rest cadence that allowed us to paddle for a long time without tiring. We had also developed the practice of pushing ourselves to ramming speed at the end of each paddle, to build up our endurance and speed in case we ever had to outrace the weather back to shore (which, I might add, we did a time or two).

All of this meant that I was particular about whom I paddled with. But then it hit me: I could get a solo boat of some sort. It needed to be light enough for me to mount on top of my car by myself, be big enough to hold a dog or two, and have space for cargo. I thought I would like a kayak.

I began searching for the right boat shortly after Gary died. It was summer, and I felt almost desperate to show myself that there was still life to be lived. I needed to know that I could camp by myself. It soon became clear that any kayak I could afford, and actually lift, was not going to be big enough to carry a dog and any amount of gear. What I really needed was a solo canoe.

About three weeks after Gary died, I loaded up Bayley and my camping gear, left the other dogs in the care of a house-sitter, and headed to Inlet, in the Adirondacks, with some friends. My plan was to buy a new canoe, while my friends planned to buy new kayaks for their family. Then I wanted to head to Stillwater Reservoir, where Gary and I had camped together many times, while my friends went to their family home in Newcomb.

"I want a light solo canoe that can carry me, my dog, and camping gear," I explained.

I had my eye on a little green canoe that was about twelve feet long. It looked perfect. I asked to try it.

"I don't think this is the one you want," the salesperson said. "I don't think it will track very well for you with that much weight in the boat."

I nodded, but really liked the look of the little boat and still wanted to try it. Thankfully, they were right next to Fifth Lake, so Bayley and I headed across the road and into the boat. I briefly pondered what paddle to try, but then thought, *Why not try a kayak paddle?*

Since Gary had always been the stern man in the canoe, I had never really learned to be proficient at steering. The kayak paddle worked great. The boat didn't. I typically like to have my dogs ride in front of me so I know what they are doing. With Bayley in the front, the boat zigzagged wildly. Clearly the woman was right.

"I think you might like this boat," the woman said as I brought the little green canoe back to the store parking lot. It was a thirty-three-pound, sixteen-foot, skin-coated solo Wenonah Kevlar canoe. Bayley and I took it for a spin. It was perfect.

In the meantime, my friends were buying four kayaks and loading them on top of their van. The van and boats were a work of art, with kayaks on top and hanging off the side of their vehicle!

"Why don't you come with us, Betsy?" Pat and Jay asked. "Honestly, we are not wild about you going off camping by yourself. Do you have any pepper spray?" they asked.

"Yes," I lied, and they, somewhat relieved, headed toward Newcomb, while Bayley and I headed to Stillwater Reservoir. I really needed to make this camping trip on my own.

I still find it hard to describe what happened on that trip. It was a mixture of spiritual renewal and a bit of weirdness.

Bayley and I put in near a restaurant located on the reservoir and headed for the place where Gary and I typically camped. It was partway up a mountain, just off a climbing trail, and quite secluded. It was strange to be there alone. The silence was almost overwhelming.

I pitched my tent, selected the dry food I wanted to fix for dinner, prepped it, and, as had been Gary's and my custom, climbed into my new boat with Bayley for a quiet early-evening paddle while the freeze-dried meal became edible food. As I set off, I saw a still partially downy duckling and its mother just offshore. As I started to paddle, the duckling came swimming confidently toward my canoe, while its mother quacked a warning a bit further off. For the next half hour, I talked with this little duckling swimming within arm's reach of my canoe.

"Hi," I said.

"Peep, peep," the duckling answered.

"My husband just died," I explained.

"Peep, peep," the duckling responded.

Suddenly I had the strangest thought. This duckling looked to be about three weeks old, the same length of time Gary had been dead.

"Are you Gary?" I asked.

"Peep, peep," the duckling said, as he swam even nearer to my boat, his mother quacking desperately several yards away.

I can only say that I felt peacefulness creep into my bones as the duckling and I paddled about together. Then, all of the

Betsy and Bayley

sudden, I had a horrible thought. *What if a snapping turtle or some other predator gets this little duck?* I shuddered.

"Gary," I said, "please be safe. I need to go back to the campsite now." It was getting late, and my food was waiting for me.

As if he had understood, the duckling gave one more peep and headed straight for his mother.

I will admit I cried a little, feeling strangely like I had both seen and lost Gary again, but most of all, I felt like I had been given a gift.

As I was trying to reconcile my grief with my joy, I approached my landing spot at the base of the mountain. I simply could not believe my eyes: There on the rock, in the evening sun, were five otters sunning themselves.

I approached slowly and silently with Bayley, and we sat totally still as we watched this family. They spotted me after a bit, and gradually eased themselves into the water. As I brought my boat in to land, I turned to watch the otters as each lifted itself partway out of the water, in a telescoping fashion, to wish me a final goodbye.

Oh, I thought. *Gary is not only the duckling; he is now part of all nature.*

It was a comforting and mystical thought.

The experience at Stillwater Reservoir changed me. I knew that I was still alive. I could still laugh. I could still cry. I could still experience joy. And maybe, just maybe, I could still experience Gary as I experienced the natural world.

❄ ❄ ❄

In late January, Bayley and I were headed out to the garage when I heard what sounded like screaming. I looked up as a fox tore around the edge of my garage, just feet away. She was running and screaming, and for a brief moment I thought that was all there was to see. Then another fox, absolutely beautiful, slightly smaller than the first, came around the corner of the garage and stopped not ten feet from Bayley and me. I froze. Bayley froze. The fox froze.

For several seconds, we all stared at each other. I was moved beyond words as we stood there, stuck in time. It was magical and beautiful. My fanciful side will always believe it was a visit from Gary. My more rational side believes it was a dog fox chasing a vixen in heat. Whatever the case, the image of that beautiful fox is burned into my memory.

❄ ❄ ❄

Since I seem to be stuck in memories that reassured me of Gary's presence after his death, there is another, but this one was connected with a human, not an animal.

I taught graduate-level courses to students who generally were working toward their counseling or school psychology degrees. One summer I was teaching a course on learning theory, when a student who was taking the course as an elective, and was not part of my program, quietly and somewhat hesitantly approached me during a break.

"Could I talk with you?" she asked.

"Of course," I replied.

"I am afraid you will think I am crazy, but I really feel I need to tell you something."

I did not really know this student well and wondered what she might tell me that would make me think she was crazy.

"Ever since I was a little girl, I have seen things other people don't see."

She had my attention, but I had no idea where this was going.

"For the past three weeks, I have seen a figure behind you, and he would talk to me," she said. "He wanted me to give you a message. I told him I would not give you a message until he totally showed himself to me. Today, he did. He was tall, with black hair and a beard. He told me that he wanted you to know that he was sorry he had to leave you, and that he is glad that you have been able to move on with your life. He wanted you to know that he loves you. Do you know who that is?" she asked.

I felt goosebumps form on my arms. I was struggling with what to say. As far as I knew, this student had no knowledge of my personal life, as her only connection with our department had been to take my summer class as an elective for a totally different graduate degree. I could think of very few ways that her telling me this would have benefited her, but certainly ways that it could have annoyed or angered me. To me, it seemed like she had taken quite a risk in telling me.

"He told me that there is a place in your woods where you can come and he thinks he might be able to talk with you there," she finished.

"Thank you for telling me," I said, as calmly and unemotionally as I could. My mind was reeling, both hopeful and skeptical at the same time. She wrote down for me all that she remembered him saying to her, and I still have her list. I asked her a few days later if she was still seeing the man in my class. "No," she said. "He was here every day until I talked with you, and I have not seen him again."

I admit I was a little disappointed. I liked the notion that he was always looking over my shoulder. I am still looking for that place in my woods but have never been sure what I would do if I thought I had found it. I suspect that I am afraid to try too hard. I like feeling like it is still out there for me to find.

Chapter 16

Sierra

While Sierra was the last dog to join the Waterman family, she quickly adapted to her new surroundings. She began to learn she now had a job and, as is often the case with Border Collies, she took it very seriously. She was fast and steady and readily trained to the task of skijoring as if she were born for the job. She would joyfully leap to her feet as soon as she saw her harness come out. She ran easily on any team with a single focus, seeming to barely notice that she was part of a team, her focus was so intent on the task at hand.

On one occasion, after Gary's death, I took Ichabod, Casper, and Sierra to a race in the eastern part of our state. Max, the son of a friend, who was a master cross-country skier, decided to try skijoring with me. We decided that with his skill and Sierra's strong work ethic and joy of running, I would run with Ichabod and Casper, and Max would run with Sierra alone.

The day of the race arrived. I was alarmed when I got to the racing trails. They were almost solid ice.

"I'm not sure that I'm comfortable racing on these trails," I said. "There is nothing for the skis to bite into. I would be totally at the mercy of my dogs."

We briefly considered withdrawing from the race, but the dogs were excited to get going, we had driven a fair distance to get there, and we both rather liked speed, so we decided to give it a try.

As the racing order came out, it turned out that Max and Sierra would go off first. Ichabod, Casper, and I would be about three teams back. This seemed okay, as Max was a great skier, and Sierra was confident and fast.

"5 – 4 – 3 – 2 – 1! Go driver!"

And Max was off and out of sight around the first turn. Two other teams took off, and then it was my turn.

"5 – 4 – 3 – 2 – 1! Go driver!" and I, too, was off. As I rounded the first turn, I was surprised to see Max and Sierra stopped a bit off the trail.

I called to Max, "What happened? What's wrong?"

"She just plain won't go," he shouted back.

As I approached, Sierra jumped forward in her harness and fell in beside my team, the team she had so often run beside in practice. We stayed in this position for the duration of the race, except when one of my skis flew off my boot and slid several feet down the icy trail. My dogs and Sierra briefly stopped while I hopped down the trail to retrieve my ski and, with considerable difficulty, got it back on my boot. All this time I was trying to stay upright on one leg with my team trying to get back on the trail and run, excited by the teams that were passing us. Max had to wait, too, as Sierra was not going anywhere without her mates. Neither Sierra nor my team would move ahead or behind the other team, and we filled up the whole trail.

Unfortunately, the race teams had to run back along the same trail they had gone out on—the one Max, our dogs, and I totally filled at this point. As you might imagine, losing my ski had set us back quite a bit, so many teams were headed back our way. And it was incredibly icy, making head-on passing nearly impossible and dangerous. When we spotted people headed toward us, we would do our best to move both our teams as far to the right as possible. Sometimes we managed a clean pass; sometimes the pass was pretty messy, almost heart-stopping. I remember one skier jumping over a bale of hay that lined the trail in an effort to avoid us. This is not easy to do with skis on and a dog pulling gamely out front. He made the jump, reentered the trail, and continued on his way. Max and I both managed to finish the race alive, a somewhat amazing outcome.

This was also the trip where we were staying at the family home of one of Max's parents, and Ichabod managed to steal and gobble down two pounds of very expensive bacon intended for our breakfast—but that is another story altogether. Max's parents still bring that up from time to time.

Sometime after Gary's death, Sierra, although gentle and responsive to me, became increasingly more aggressive toward the other dogs. Bayley and Casper just ignored her when she would raise her lip at them, but Ichabod and Neeka clearly did not like it. One time too many, Sierra raised her lip at the Huskies, and both Ichabod and Neeka came after her. Anyone that has seen a dogfight knows just how scary they can be.

I was terrified and knew I had to get them apart. This was not just posturing. The three dogs were seriously fighting. Sierra, although she had started it, was going to be killed if we didn't intervene. I had remarried by this time and, thankfully, Dave was there as well. We both ran into the fray and managed to get them separated before too much damage was done, although there was blood on Sierra. Our peaceful kennel of dogs was no longer one we could trust if we were not there.

We sought the help of a respected local dog trainer. He worked with us and with Sierra, but his advice was to never let the Huskies be alone with Sierra again. He said the Huskies had clearly told us that they did not want her in their family, and his fear was, if we were not there to stop it, that they might succeed in killing her. We were able to build another adjoining fence so Sierra was near the others during the day and could enter the dog room directly into her kennel, without having direct contact with the other dogs. For many years, however, the dogs continued to sleep in one room, peacefully, with us. That all changed one day, when Dave and I were away.

We got a call from Becky, our competent dog sitter, that Gracie (more about her later), a young Alaskan Husky we had been given by a friend, had gotten into a fight with Sierra in the bedroom. Neither dog was very hurt, but Becky, who was reluctant to tell us this, had been bitten by Sierra as she moved in to separate the two. We felt terrible that Becky had been bitten, and surprised when she was still willing to dog-sit for us after that. From that time on, we would bring Sierra up by herself and spend some time with her, before putting her in the master bathroom to stay safely away from the Huskies at night. Amazingly, though, she never lifted her lip at them if she was under harness, and we continued to run her with one of the Huskies from time to time. Something about having a clear job to do seemed to remove the animosity the dogs had for each other.

Sierra lived to be fifteen years old and became completely blind. She knew her way around the house and moved fairly freely, even in her blindness. While she could be a bit of a nuisance with the other dogs, I will always remember the wonderful hugs she would give me. As I leaned over, she would place her front paws around my neck, snuggle her head in next to my body, and hold on as I lifted her completely off the floor in my arms.

Chapter 17

Casper

Casper was our serious one. He enjoyed a good game of fetch, but even that seemed to be a type of work for him. Enjoyable work, but work, nonetheless. He was always watching, trying to know what he was supposed to do next. Over time, he became quite a talented Frisbee dog.

A nearby city holds a harbor festival each year, and one year they had a man who presented shows with his professional Frisbee Dogs. I wanted to go watch them, and I wanted to take Casper along. I thought he might enjoy watching too. The show was delightful, and after the show I walked, with Casper, up to thank the man and tell him how much I had enjoyed the show.

"Does your Border Collie like to catch Frisbees?" he asked.

"Yes," I said. "But we don't do fancy stuff like you do."

"Well, let's see," he said, and proceeded to throw a Frisbee up in the air. Casper jumped, turning his body expertly as he cleanly caught the Frisbee.

"Wow!" the man said. "It would not take much to train him. He's a natural."

For the next few minutes, the man gently worked with my dog. Casper was enjoying his moment as a small group of people came to watch.

One woman said, "Oh, I am so glad that I caught a part of the show. I was afraid it would be over by the time I got here."

It was, of course, but she never knew it. Casper and I were both proud that for one brief moment, Casper was part of a very talented troupe of dogs.

A mushing friend called Dave and me one day and said, "I have the perfect skijoring dog for you. Gracie is too small for my team but is an excellent leader and very fast. She's a little shy, but she loves to run. I think she'd make a good partner for Casper."

My immediate reaction was to say no. We had five dogs at that point, and that seemed enough. It is also sometimes difficult to add a new dog to an established group. Her dogs, while well cared for, also generally lived outdoors, and were not necessarily housebroken. I worried that could be an issue for us, as our dogs were more house dogs than mushing dogs. Before I could say no, however, she suggested, "How about you try her out with Casper?"

I am always up for a good skijor run, so we loaded up our dogs and headed up east. Dave took Ichabod and Sierra, a good team in their own right, and I hooked up Casper and Gracie. We flew. It was likely the best run of my life. Her dog had done a lot of training and was in great shape, and Casper was fast and steady.

I simply couldn't say no, so we were back to a six-dog household. Casper and Gracie were exceptional at running together. And at almost every race, someone would offer—sometimes kidding and sometimes seriously—to buy Gracie.

Gracie would get extremely excited as she waited for her turn to come to the start line. Casper was always excited, too, but his excitement showed itself in extreme focus. He would stand totally still, sometimes quivering a bit, and stare at the start line, almost rigid. Gracie, however, was in constant motion as she waited to start. The problem, of course, was that the two dogs were hooked *together* to a tug line, with their two lines coming out of a single line that attached to my waist. One wanted to stand still while he waited, and one practically could not stop moving.

In her excitement, Gracie would begin to jump back and forth right over Casper's back. Casper would tolerate this for a few minutes before he would turn his head to her and give a short growl, as if to say, "Grow up and stop jumping. We have serious stuff to do here today." A kind of doggie correction, if you will. Gracie would seem a bit startled by his crankiness and would stop her jumping briefly, only to start again, until Casper could stand it no longer and would snap at her again.

This pattern to starting a race was very entertaining to those watching, a little annoying to me, and very annoying to Casper. But once we were underway, the dogs moved together as if in a single motion, all crankiness pushed aside as they did what they loved to do. We would run silently through the beautiful winter snow, all of us smiling.

There were also times when I ran Casper and Sierra together, a beautiful Border Collie team. They had quickly learned the important terms and knew which way to go when we called out "haw" for left or "gee" for right. The dogs, in fact, were more solid on these terms than I was. I have always been a bit handicapped when it came to consistently using the terms "right" and "left," often misspeaking. It wasn't that I didn't know my left from my right. It was more of a linguistics thing. When I was giving directions, people quickly learned to question what direction I might really mean. This was also the case with the dogs. Casper in particular, when I called out "gee" or "haw," would turn his head slightly toward me to see if I really meant what I was saying. He would get a glimpse of my body position, see that I really meant "haw" this time, and swing confidently toward the left. Or, alternatively, he would see that I really meant "gee" this time and swing toward the right, regardless of my misspoken command. He didn't seem particularly distressed about my mistakes; he just learned how to compensate for them, something I am still trying to do.

Casper and Sierra also knew that "whoa" meant to slow up, "on by" meant to move past another team or some other distraction that might present itself on the trail, "wait" meant to hold in one place, "leave it" meant to ignore some distracting thing—disgusting or otherwise—that might be in front of them, and "come around"—an important command—meant to bring the team around and head in the other direction. I never really knew if my Huskies had actually learned these commands, as they simply always followed the lead of the Border Collies.

A friend, Jane (in fact, the person who had given us Gracie), was training a young, inexperienced, four-dog sled dog team when she gave me a call. It was in the early days of winter and, while there was snow on the trails, it was not deep enough to set a snow hook, a device attached to the back of the sled that acts a bit like an emergency brake for a dogsled. Each time she needed to turn her team around to head back to her truck, she had to get off the back of her sled, grab the lines of her dogs who were still pulling forward, grab the two

Betsy racing in a storm

lead dogs, bring them around so that they were headed in the opposite direction, continue to hold onto the lines as she worked her way back to the sled, and climb back on. All in all, a bit of a risky procedure with inexperienced dogs, as a quick jump forward by the team could send the musher flying, and the team would be off without any human guiding them.

In fact, a very experienced musher, skijorer, and friend once lost his ten-dog team as he was just about to set out on a training run. He had his team fastened to his truck when the dogs lunged forward. The carabiner holding them to the truck snapped, and the dogs were off, down an unplowed road. The musher gave chase, but it quickly became clear that he could not catch them on foot. He jumped in his truck and drove on plowed roads to a place where the trail the dogs were running on intersected with his road. There was no sign of them. He called Dave and me, hoping we might be able to help him track them. We took our skijor teams, called a few more friends, and we all went out to search.

We were all worried. If the dogs somehow got off the trail, they could quickly become caught up in brush and downed trees. The dogs were linked together, so they could not escape each other, and might attack each other in their fright and attempt to get free.

As we were asking snowmobilers coming up a trail where we thought the dogs might be running, one man said he had seen a large free team coming up Bargey Road, and that he had tried to jump on the back of the sled, but that they were going too fast, and he was thrown off before he got his footing. He said they had made a left turn down a plowed road and that he had lost sight of them. We didn't know whether to believe him or not, but it gave us a place to start looking. We searched most of the afternoon, until night fell. Sadly, we all went home, our worry for the safety of Roy's dogs increasing.

The next morning, we were back out looking. The area where the dogs were running was huge in terms of square miles. It was impossible for us to search all of the areas, especially since much of it is inaccessible by truck or car. We needed more help. I had an idea.

"What if we call several radio and TV stations and ask for help from snowmobilers?" I asked. "We could make a grid of the area and assign different people to different areas," I finished.

This was still a long shot, as there was no assurance that the dogs had stayed on a trail, but it seemed better than what we were doing.

While the others continued searching, I went home and made some calls, explaining the importance of finding the dogs as quickly as possible. All of the radio and TV stations were willing to put the message in their news segments. A person at one of the stations, however, made an additional suggestion:

"Why don't you try calling the DEC?" he asked. "They may be able to help organize a search."

What a great idea, I thought, and called New York State Department of Environmental Conservation right away.

The first question the DEC asked was more difficult to answer than I would have imagined.

"What county are they in?" the man asked. "So we know which people to get involved."

We live near the border of two counties, and it was impossible to know which one the dogs were in at this point. *Was this going to be a stopper?* I wondered.

The man seemed to grasp the seriousness of the situation in terms of the dogs' safety, and said, to my amazement, "Maybe the State Police will be willing to get involved. We have a much better chance of finding them if they can go up in a helicopter."

I couldn't imagine that was even possible, but he told me he would call me back once he had talked with the State Police. I waited for his return call.

Only a few minutes passed before I got a call back.

"They have a helicopter in the air and are headed to where you said someone might have last seen the dogs."

I might have teared up a little at this news; I jumped into my car and headed back up to the Tug. Cell phone connections there are very weak and mostly absent, so I was surprised when I got a call from a DEC officer within minutes of getting into my car.

"The State Police have located the dogs and are hovering over where they are," he said. "We are sending a car up there to assist." (I am actually crying as I write this.)

At this point, I was the only person who had this information. Those still searching knew only that I was planning to call the radio and TV stations to ask for help. I needed to get information to the searchers as quickly as I could. As I approached the area, I spotted Roy's truck and let him know that the State Police had found the dogs and were hovering over them in a helicopter. We both drove closer to Bargey Road and spotted the helicopter. I also saw Dave's vehicle and a dog truck being driven by another pair of searchers. I alerted them to what was going on.

The DEC officers had already arrived and had walked back into the woods to the dogs. Roy was on his way to his dogs, running as fast as he could. Knowing how much Roy loved his dogs, we were hesitant to ask the question.

"What condition are they in?" we asked, knowing they had been gone for over thirty-six hours at that point.

"Most look pretty good," the DEC officer said, "but one is dead."

We gasped. Dave looked at me and began running back, trying to catch up with Roy. While Roy can sound tough at times, he loves his dogs with a great fierceness, and we knew that finding any dogs dead or injured would be devastating for him.

Within a few minutes, Dave was walking out carrying the dead dog.

"It was a good thing I got back there when I did," he said. He had found Roy kneeling beside the dead dog, grieving. Dave quickly cut the dead dog loose from the line with his pocketknife and reminded Roy that he needed to tend to the others, trying to break through his grief.

Another couple helping us search was much more prepared than we were. We had not really thought about how we would get the dogs separated from each other or how we would get them back to a truck. Our focus had been on finding them. They, however, had brought some cutting tools and several leashes, and were racing back to help Roy.

The State Police helicopter, which had hovered over the dogs until they saw us reach them, waved a quick goodbye and was off. It made for a pretty good news story, and two TV stations sent reporters out to interview Roy at his home.

"One died," he said sadly to the reporter, "but nine were checked out by my vet and are okay."

It would take some considerable retraining for the dogs to become comfortable pulling as a team again, but they did, and both Roy and his dogs were able to again feel the surge of joy that comes with running silently through the wooded trails together.

We are forever thankful to the DEC and the State Police for their critical roles in saving these dogs.

But back to my original story. Jane feared losing her team during a training session and called me.

"Could I borrow Casper and Sierra to lead my team in some training runs?" she asked.

"Of course," I said, feeling a bit proud of my dogs.

For several days, she would come and pick up my dogs, place them in the lead position on her team, take her run, and then bring the dogs back to me after an hour or two.

"Come around," she would call. And these two little Border Collies would bring her team of strong Huskies around so that they were headed in the opposite direction—without Jane having to leave her spot behind the sled. All in all, a much safer way to turn her team.

I don't remember if we finally had enough snow for her to set her hook, or if her dogs learned how to "come around" from the Borders, but after a couple of weeks, Jane was on her own again, and my dogs were back running silently on the trails with me.

Casper was always a dog that seemed focused on knowing what he was supposed to do, and he seldom broke any of our household rules. He had never tried to get out of the yard and when he was not on leash, I could totally depend on his recall. Because he was such a dependable dog, I was shocked one day when I called the dogs to come in, as a noisy thunderstorm was bearing down on us, and Casper was not with the others as they bounded in from our fenced yard. All of my Border Collies were terrified of thunderstorms, while the Huskies seemed to take them in stride. The storm that day had both strong winds and lots of heavy thunder and lightning.

When Casper didn't come inside with the others, I feared he might have been injured by a falling branch or tree in the yard. I called a friend, fearing I might need help if he was injured, and the two of us searched every inch of the two-acre fenced yard. Still no sign of Casper. I was near panic. I had no idea where to look or exactly what to do. He had never, ever wandered away.

My friend and I searched and called, and we could not find any sign of Casper. It was several hours after the storm, and I had called everyone I could think to call, when my phone rang.

A man asked, "Are you missing a Border Collie?" My heart rose.

"Yes!" I said anxiously.

"Well he is here in my garage. My wife found him hiding in my garage and shut him in because she thought I had brought home another dog. She wasn't very happy with me," he explained. "She never even looked to see that he had tags."

"Where do you live?" I asked, expecting that he lived somewhere on my street.

"I am over on Ridge Road," he said.

Somehow Casper had been so terrified by the storm that he had managed to escape the fence, run across a major four-lane highway, and end up, frightened, in someone else's garage, almost four miles from my home. We never did learn how he got out or how he ran so far. I just know that it had to be a terrifying experience for him, and we were both glad he was home.

Casper was slowing down as he aged, and we had long since given up racing. He was fourteen years old and had lost some of his hearing, but still enjoyed an easy game of fetch. One morning when we awoke, Casper seemed to be having trouble walking. He would list into the walls and seemed confused, not seeming to even recognize his name or us. Something had clearly happened in the night. We called the vet.

When we arrived, Casper could barely walk, so we carried him into the examination room.

The veterinarian examined him and said, "It looks like he has suffered a stroke."

Together, we decided it was time to say goodbye. Casper was never very big in stature, weighing slightly less than forty pounds at his heaviest, but his heart and commitment to his family and his jobs were legendary.

Chapter 18

Ichabod, the Escape Artist

Ichabod was particularly challenging as he was always looking for a way to go for a run. He was quick, and he was
determined. Once, before Gary got sick, we had taken all five
of our dogs to visit our daughter in Cape Cod. Her yard was
large and fenced in for her two Border Collies, and all of the
dogs enjoyed playing together. We were careful and tried to
keep a close eye on Ichabod as, by now, we knew he was a
gifted escape artist. He was always watching for a chance to
run free.

This day, someone took just a second too long to close
the front door, and Ichabod was out in a flash. We gave chase
on foot, but that only seemed to encourage him. Gary got in
the car and tried to coax him in, too, but he would look and
then run merrily away. Gary feared he was making matters
worse, chasing him further and further away, so he returned
to Amy's house and we waited, wondering exactly what to do.
Gary figured Ichabod was two or three miles up the road by
the time he had turned the car around, and we were sure we
had lost him this time.

After an hour or so had passed, we looked out into Amy's
front yard, and there was Ichabod, waiting to be let back into
the house. It was so much like the run he had taken from our

house on the first day we had him. Somehow, he knew how to get back to the place he had left, even when he had never been to that place before. We let him in, breathed a big sigh of relief, and promised each other that we would be even more vigilant.

Ichabod had a thing for bread, and, ultimately, we learned if we had bread in our hands, he would come running back. But you had to be careful—he was big and strong and could snatch it out of your hand and go back to running if you didn't have a good hold on his collar before giving him the bread. And he could recognize bread no matter how it was camouflaged. He would grab a loaf of bread off of the counter, rip the plastic off in a flash, and gobble as fast as he could until someone intervened. You had to guard your sandwiches, or he might snatch them off your plate.

One day, we brought some bread home from a restaurant, wrapped in aluminum foil, and almost before we got in the door, he snatched the bread from our hands, removed the foil, and swallowed the bread in one gulp. We wondered about his extreme fondness for bread and then realized he had been found behind a restaurant that served bread with every meal and disposed of the leftover bread in a large trash container behind the restaurant. We will never know for sure, but we suspect he may have lived for months off the bread he found there when he was living alone on the streets.

We were always trying to find a way to make a more secure fence. Gary had made the ten-acre invisible fence, which was perfect for the Border Collies, but not for the Huskies. We knew we had to do something different.

We had lots of dogs and lots of land, but a six-foot hard fence of any size seemed beyond our means. A friend mentioned one day that strings of regular electrified pasture fence had worked well for them and was a fairly inexpensive setup. We put in fence posts and ran several lines of wire, about six inches or so apart, horizontally. All in all, we enclosed about two acres of land behind our house. It was this fence that Ichabod had reentered when he returned after his first day with us, surely getting shocked as he did. For the most part, this arrangement worked—the dogs had a large area, were separated from the front of the house, and were not always in the water. We had to be vigilant, though, making sure no tree limbs had fallen and damaged the lines, but it worked quite well, even with the Huskies.

When Gary died, I was nervous about maintaining the fencing lines, as I knew little about how to fix them should they fail. I decided to have a large five-foot chain-link fence installed that could connect to my back deck. I felt much better seeing this secure space for them, and relieved that it was not so vulnerable to damage from falling branches.

The dogs had a routine at feeding time that was entertaining to watch. Each dog had a different room, with their bowl of food ready for them when they came in. We had learned early on that feeding them all in the same room meant Neeka would bolt down her food and then bully the other dogs away from theirs so she could eat it. Each dog quickly learned which room was their own, and each would run directly to their space—one in the kitchen, one in the main bathroom, one in the office, one in the office waiting room, one in the master bathroom, and Ichabod in the master bedroom. Getting to the bedroom meant that Ichabod had to take a sharp turn out of the kitchen and down a hallway. He came in at such breathtaking speed that he learned he could bank off the doorway frame and slide the rest of the way to the bedroom. We actually had people come to visit just to see Ichabod fly.

Ichabod's ability to escape became rather legendary, and while we worked diligently to prevent it, it was always an uphill battle. I was walking him with a friend's dog around our property on a retractable leash when he made a quick turn and pulled. The leash popped out of my hand. He was off into the woods. By this time, I had realized that when Ichabod escaped, it meant he would run for a few minutes and then come back for some bread. This time, though, I was very worried. Much of our property is covered with low brush, and the type of leash he had on could easily get caught, keeping him trapped. We searched. We called. I had visions of Ichabod caught and unable to return. Several hours went by. Then a night went by. I was frantic.

My friend came again the next day with her dog. It seemed rather futile, but we kept searching. I thought we might hear him bark or jump around if he was caught, but we heard no sounds. Suddenly my friend's dog stopped and stood completely still. We looked in the direction her dog was looking and, just barely, we saw Ichabod. He was so caught up in brush and small tree branches that he could not even lie down. Strangely, he made no sound or movement. Without my friend's dog alerting us to something, we would surely have walked right past him, and he could have died a horrible death. I was shaking as I released him, realizing, once again, that Ichabod was a dog with many lives.

Ichabod's days of escaping were still not over. I had the solid fence in and had even added some strings of electric wire to the top to make it more secure, since Ichabod seemed able to get over nearly everything. But still he was escaping. We checked the fence. It was not damaged. We were perplexed until one day I looked out at the yard and couldn't believe my eyes. I watched as Ichabod climbed partway up the fence and then jumped to a limb on a nearby tree. He balanced there for a moment, his feet in a single, narrow line on the small branch. He rocked slightly back and forth as he gained his balance, and then nimbly jumped over the fence, clearing the electric wires quite neatly. Then he was off. Now that we knew his means of escape, we could take action. Dave, whom I had married a few years after Gary's death, took out the chainsaw and cut off the branch. It was almost sad to see Ichabod try over and over to find the branch that was now missing. Almost.

Probably the funniest thing I ever witnessed was coming home from work and being met at the door by Gracie, an Alaskan Husky who was given to Dave and me by a mushing friend, some years after Gary had died. I was puzzled. How did she get into the house? What I found downstairs when I went to check on the rest of the dogs, though, was downright hilarious. Dave had built an addition to the house, and under it he built a room leading directly into their fenced yard. The dogs could enter and leave through a dog door. This room was closed off to the rest of the house by a regular external door while we were at work. Ichabod had somehow learned to pull the handle down and toward him, letting himself, and all of the other dogs, into the basement. We could see the teeth marks on the handle where he had clearly been practicing. Gracie, the only dog who had gotten past the basement, had done so by somehow squeezing herself through the small cat door between the basement and the first floor.

Neeka, though, won the prize for the funniest. As I came down to a basement full of dogs, Neeka was looking at me through a fish-bowl-like treat container. She had stuck her head into the container, eaten all of treats it contained, and was looking exactly like I would imagine a doggie astronaut on Mars might look. I would have run back up to get a camera, and honestly I still wish I had, but I was afraid she might be without enough air. Neeka, however, was totally calm, like having a treat container on her head was an everyday occurrence. It took some effort to get it off, but she didn't seem to mind. We fixed the problem with Ichabod and his ability to open doors by putting up a sign next to the door reminding us to "ALWAYS LOCK THIS DOOR!"

❄ ❄ ❄

I was racing with Ichabod and Casper one January day. We were running our dogs in a race sponsored by the Pennsylvania Sled Dog Club but held only twenty minutes or so from our house. Just as I was getting to the start line, ready to race, a man approached me.

Crossing the finish line

"Where did you get that dog?" he asked, pointing to Ichabod. I gulped.

Oh no, I thought. *Is this the owner who had lost Ichabod?*

But I was racing next, so he said, "I'll talk with you when you get back."

Races are fun. They take you through the forest, up and down hills, and past some cheering people. But this time I was worried. What would I say if he said this was his dog? I'd had Ichabod for several years by this point, and he was an important member of my family.

"No," I decided as we raced along. "I will not let him take Ichabod away."

I held my breath as I crossed the finish line and saw the man waiting for me. He came over, congratulated me on my run, and said, "Let me tell you a story about this dog."

As it turned out, he wasn't telling me a story about Ichabod specifically, but about where he was convinced Ichabod had come from.

"You see those particular spots on his face?" he asked. "And his particular build and coloring?"

Indeed, I saw those things. Ichabod had always been a bit of a unique-looking dog.

"He is out of a particular breeding of dog that was developed in Alaska. Very long-legged, rather thin, with long noses and unique coloring. Where did you get him?"

It didn't really sound like a threat, just curiosity.

"We found him at a shelter in Pulaski," I answered. "He had clearly been a sled dog and a good leader. He knew what he was doing from the moment we brought him home."

"Someone lost a good dog," he said. "And you got a good dog. I expect he started his life in Alaska."

I breathed a sigh of relief.

❄ ❄ ❄

We, of course, didn't know Ichabod's actual age, but he was fully grown when we got him. One day, as Dave and I were returning from a trip to Houston by car, we got a call from our dog-sitter. She was clearly upset.

"I don't know how to tell you this," she said. "I came down to feed the dogs tonight, and Ichabod was dead." He had not acted ill, she explained, and had seemed fine when she fed the dogs in the morning.

We were getting fairly close to home after our long trip, and finished the final leg in record time, arriving rather late at night. We wrapped Ichabod in a blanket and moved him out of the dog room, waiting to bury him in the morning.

We'd had him for thirteen years.

Chapter 19

Neeka

Neeka, like Ichabod, was an escape artist. She, however, dug under fences, while Ichabod sailed over them. Gary was home for a brief respite from the hospital when Neeka came up missing. I was working, but Gary started looking and calling for her. He came back into the house to get the keys to the car to look further, when the phone rang.

"Do you own a red Husky?" the voice asked.

Gulp!

"Yes we do," he answered.

"Well, she just killed my pet rooster," came the reply.

We felt horrible. What do you say? What can you do?

Gary drove over to pick up Neeka. He felt terribly sad, embarrassed, and guilty about what had happened, and tried to pay the woman for what Neeka had done.

"There is no need to pay me. I am just very sad about what happened. I also know that you are going through a very hard time. Please don't worry too much about it."

But we did. We really needed to find a better way to keep our dogs in. We looked for holes under the fence and filled them with rocks. We were as vigilant as we could be. Years went by, and Neeka did not escape. Although she tried to dig under the fence, we had filled all the holes, and we hoped she would quit trying.

One night, a few years after Gary died, I called the dogs in for dinner. Everyone came running except Neeka. That was unusual, as she loved dinner. Dave and I went out to call her. Nothing. Clearly, she had somehow escaped again. We fed the rest of the dogs and then went looking for Neeka. We called. We walked through our woods and up the road a bit. Then a horrible thought occurred to me.

The county fair was in full swing at the fairgrounds, just over the hill from our house. This meant lots of people and a lot of animals.

"Oh no! I said to Dave. "What if Neeka found her way to the fair and got into one of the poultry buildings?"

We gave each other a horrified look, got in the car, and drove into the fairgrounds. It was after 11:30 p.m. by this time, and the fairgrounds were eerily quiet. We parked our car and quietly walked into the grounds. We looked into the poultry building and gave a sigh of relief. No sign of any destruction there. We walked into the rabbit building. Nothing. The sheep and goats building. Nothing. The cattle building. Nothing.

"Okay," I said. "She's definitely not here."

We resumed our search, driving slowly up our road. We drove by the log cabin near our house. It sits quite a way back from the road.

"Stop," I called. "I think I saw something on their porch."

Slowly we backed up, and we could just make out the silhouette of a dog. *Our* dog. Now how do we get her to come to our car without frightening the people living there? We were uncomfortable walking down their long driveway, as we feared they might think we were trying to break into their

Neeka

house. Calling loudly to Neeka also seemed like a problem. We opted to try whispering. "Neeka. Here, girl."

She noticed us and had just stood up when our neighbor opened her door, probably because there was a car with lights on lingering on the road outside of her house.

Neeka sprang into action, rushing to the door. The woman, not expecting a large dog on her porch, screamed and slammed the door in Neeka's face. Neeka seemed a bit put off as she came trotting up to the car and jumped in. We whispered, "Sorry! Sorry!" to our poor neighbor and slowly drove away.

One morning Dave and I were hanging out with the dogs when Neeka started to act strangely. She went limp and seemed unable to move. It almost appeared that her airway had closed off. It was off-hours for our vet, but we called, described what we were seeing, and quickly carried Neeka to the car. During the twenty-minute drive, Neeka began to come around, and sat up rather perkily on the seat. The vet met us at the door, expecting the worst. Neeka looked totally fine.

That was the first of many seizures Neeka was to have. The vet gave us some medications and, for the most part, they helped to limit the occurrences.

Neeka still enjoyed skijoring, and the exercise did not seem at all connected with her seizures, so we continued modest training. Dave, by this time, had joined me in skijoring, and typically ran Ichabod and Casper, while I ran Sierra and Neeka in races. Neeka could be a little uneven in her motivation to run. Sometimes she would run fast and steady. Other times she wanted to take a more leisurely approach to running. And anyone who has run dogs knows that if the dog isn't into running, there is really no way to make them. You are as fast as your slowest dog, the saying among mushers goes. Neeka could be quite fast, or she could also just meander along, enjoying the sights.

We were at a race, and Sierra, Neeka, and I had had a good run and were just nearing the crowd of people at the finish line. I was feeling proud of my dogs and myself for having a clean run, when a small vole ran across just in front of Neeka. In a flash—and in front of dozens of people—Neeka made a jump, not unlike those you might see from a fox in winter on the National Geographic channel, and disappeared nose-first into the snowbank. The vole won that day, and Sierra, Neeka, and I ultimately crossed the finish line, while the crowd, who had enjoyed Neeka's performance, laughed and cheered.

❄ ❄ ❄

"Betsy," Dave quietly called. "I think something is wrong with Neeka."

He had called her in for dinner, and she didn't come. His first thought was that Neeka may have escaped, although she had not been loose for many years. He went out into the fenced yard with a flashlight. Neeka was lying in one of her favorite holes and did not want to come in for the night. She looked up at us, as if begging to stay in her hole. Dave and I looked at each other. Neeka was fourteen and had been slowing down a great deal.

"I think she's dying," Dave said, sadly.

She did not seem in any pain, so we left her in her favorite spot. We covered her with a blanket and checked on her throughout the night. She seemed to be sleeping peacefully. In the morning, we planned to take her to the vet. By morning, though, Neeka had followed Ichabod and Spirit to wherever dogs go to run free.

Chapter 20

Spirit

From the first moment I saw Spirit, I fell in love with her. She was a bit shy, but there was something gentle about her that soothed my soul. I was a little worried about her, because she always seemed so reserved and quiet. The vet had assured us that she was healthy, so we had to believe that she was just a quiet dog.

As time went on, Gary and I could see that Spirit really didn't enjoy skijoring, and we wondered if she might be happier with a non-skijoring family. A wonderful friend had also fallen in love with Spirit and asked hesitantly if we might consider giving Spirit to her.

"No," I quickly answered. I couldn't imagine giving Spirit away.

Over time, though, we wondered if we weren't being selfish. Spirit got along well with all of the dogs, but she seemed to prefer lying on the couch to going on runs with the rest of them.

We called our friend. "Yes," we said. We'll let Spirit come live with you."

When our friend arrived to pick up Spirit, she showed us the new bed and toys she had purchased for her. Gary and I shed some tears and watched as Spirit left with our friend.

I immediately regretted our decision, but we knew our friend would give her a good and loving home.

About three weeks after Spirit left, we got a call from our friend. She was crying. Spirit had eaten almost nothing from the time she had left our house, and the vet told her he was concerned she might die. She had lost weight and appeared despondent.

"We are on our way," I said. Gary, Bayley, and I jumped into the car and drove the forty-five minutes to her house to pick up the dog we should have never given away.

Spirit greeted us warmly, but it was Bayley she seemed most happy to see. She leaped into our car and snuggled close to Bayley, who began to wash her face. We were all crying. I was a little embarrassed when our friend reached into the car to give Spirit a final pat, and Spirit moved as far away from her as she could, hiding behind Bayley. We knew the woman had not harmed her, but that Spirit, who had lived with a breeder, then a trainer, and then with us, simply couldn't endure another move. And there was Bayley. They had loved

Spirit and Bayley

240

each other from the first day, and after Spirit came back to live with us, the two of them were virtually inseparable.

As soon as we got home, Spirit began to eat, and her whole attitude seemed to have improved. While she was still quiet and didn't seem to enjoy the skijoring runs as much as the other dogs, she would run with us sometimes, and, in general, she seemed content just to watch and to snuggle with Bayley.

One day, after Gary had gotten sick, we noticed that Spirit was limping. We called the vet. After taking X-rays, our vet had some disturbing news. Spirit, while only three years old, had the bones of a much older dog.

"She is suffering from a degenerative bone disease, which is causing her pain," the vet explained. The only real treatment seemed to be to give her aspirin to help control the pain.

Finally, we knew, at least in part, a possible reason for her quietness and her reluctance to join the other dogs in a run. She was to live only a year from that diagnosis.

One day, about four months after Gary died, Spirit simply could not stand up. She was crying and making moaning sounds. I called the vet.

"We can try some different pain medications," she started to say. Then there was a pause. "I'm sorry, but that would be wrong," our vet continued. "While the decision is yours," she said, "you should know that she is not going to get better."

"I think we should put her down," I said, choking on my words.

We made an appointment for later in the day, as I had a client to see in the meantime.

I went into my office for the appointment, but I was struggling. My client noticed and asked what was wrong. I explained about Spirit.

We finished our time together and, hesitantly, she asked, "Would you like me to go with you to take Spirit?"

It was one of the most generous and kind things she could have said. I was struggling in my mind about ethics and boundaries, and then I said, "Yes. I would."

Spirit was only four years old.

Chapter 21

Bayley (and Gracie)

B ayley was the old dog of the crew, although all of the dogs, with the exception of Gracie, were within about one year of each other in age. Bayley was the most relaxed Border Collie I ever met. He endured horrible injuries, but never lost his love for people or for the other dogs that came to join him. As Leo lay dying, suffering pain from his bone cancer, Bayley had stayed close to him, licking his face. He was always gentle and loving. The same was true when Bayley was with Spirit. He lay with her and comforted her in much the same way he had Leo. Bayley seemed to know when one of the other dogs was in pain and would patiently lie beside them for hours.

Bayley was the peacemaker among our dogs. He would move between two of our dogs if they were playing too roughly, simply moving back and forth, preventing them from escalating their play into any kind of aggression. The other dogs seemed to respect him and generally listened to him.

Bayley, in fact, was also the song leader of our dogs. He would jump onto a small bench in the dog room, throw his head back, and we would hear, "Yip, yip, yip," which was the best he seemed able to do in terms of howling. Soon, though, all of the dogs would begin to howl together. We called it singing, and I still smile as I remember the dogs, heads together, singing their songs. Neeka was a low bass, Ichabod was more of a tenor, and the Borders would fill in the middle. It was a beautiful thing to hear.

One day I was out in the fenced area playing with my dogs. It was a place where all the dogs could run free. While I could easily take the Border Collies outside the fence to play, I didn't dare do that with the Huskies. I was running around, and they were tearing along after me, dodging trees. We were having a great time together. All of a sudden, Ichabod miscalculated a turn and ran hard into a tree. While some say dogs don't experience emotions, I saw two emotions from Ichabod that day. Unfortunately, Bayley was running very near to Ichabod when Ichabod slammed into the tree. It sure looked like anger as he lashed out at the dog nearest to him, grabbing Bayley by his leg and pulling him down. Bayley cried, and Ichabod immediately let go.

Bayley continued to cry as I went quickly to him. There was a small, superficial puncture wound where Ichabod had grabbed Bayley, and Bayley was limping. Almost as quickly as Ichabod's anger had surfaced, though, he acted remorseful, coming over to Bayley and licking his face. It looked like an apology to me, and one that, Bayley, the dog who loved and forgave everyone, accepted easily. Ichabod had injured Bayley a bit more than the small bite that was evident, and Bayley limped for several days. When I would look out into the yard over the next few days, Ichabod was almost always walking next to the dog he had hurt.

I always took Bayley with me when I would go skijoring with the other dogs, but after the first two years or so, I decided it put too much pressure on Bayley to have him pull. He always wanted to go, though, and he almost always stayed very close to the teams as we moved down the dirt roads and trails. I would love to watch him as he moved into the lead position, placing himself just in front and in the middle of the two dogs I was training. When he needed to slow his pace a bit, he was free to move over to the side where he would lope along more slowly.

I was training my second team of dogs, Sierra and Neeka, on my bicycle, when I suddenly realized that Bayley was no longer running alongside us. I remembered that he had seen a squirrel a few moments before, but he seldom gave chase for long, preferring to stay with the dogs and me. I stopped. I called. I panicked. Where had Bayley gone?

I took the dogs back to the car and started driving down the dirt road, calling out the window as I went. No sign of Bayley. I searched for as long as I could, and with a heavy heart, I called Dave, whom I had just started dating, and asked if he might be able to come search a bit while I was in class. We planned that I would join him as soon as I returned home. In a moment of brilliance, I remembered that Bayley's tag had my home telephone number on it, so before I left for class, I quickly changed my answering machine message, asking for anyone that might have found Bayley to call my cell phone.

A few minutes later, during my forty-five-minute drive to campus, my cell phone rang.

"I have your Border Collie," the man said.

I burst into tears and thanked him profusely.

"How did you find him?" I asked.

"Oh," he responded. "I didn't actually find your dog. Your dog found me. He basically chased my truck down, and when I opened the door to see why he was running alone down the road, he jumped into my truck. I looked at his tag, called the number on the tag, heard the message, and called your cell."

I was unsure exactly what to do. The man explained that he had come up to the area to hunt when he found Bayley. I didn't want to upset his plans, but I wasn't sure how to get him until after class. I asked if he might be able to tie Bayley at the home of one of my friends in the area, until I could get to him. Not an idea that I liked very much, as Bayley had never been tied, but it was the best I could think of.

This man then made a suggestion that totally erased all of the anger I had ever felt about hunters. He offered to make the twenty-minute drive to my house, put Bayley inside the door of my house, and then go back to the area to finish his hunting. I found it somehow ironic that it was a hunter who had first hurt Bayley as a six-month-old puppy, and a hunter that had rescued him as an aging dog. I knew there was a lesson in there somewhere.

Bayley was fourteen years old and had lost most of his hearing. It was not too much of a handicap, though, because Bayley was very good at keeping a close watch on his world. As he slowed down, he started to eat less and less. It was clear that he was coming near to the end of his life. He would stop eating for a few days and then rally, eating and seeming to have more energy. I have always felt very strongly that I should never let a dog suffer just to keep them with me longer, but Bayley seemed in good spirits and did not seem to be experiencing any pain, so we watched and waited, hoping we could have a bit longer with him. We were in an up cycle when I was to go with a friend to Quebec City in Canada. I was a bit reluctant to go, but Bayley seemed stronger, and I was going to be gone for only a few days. Dave promised to keep me posted if Bayley's condition worsened.

I was to return the next day when I got a call from Dave. Bayley had not eaten for several days and appeared to be getting close to death. My friend and I packed our things quickly and started the eight-hour drive back home. I rushed into the room where Bayley was lying on his bed, covered in a blanket. He appeared to be sleeping but could not be roused. Dave and I sat on the floor with him. I let him know I was home and that he was about the best dog anyone could ever have. I told him I was sorry for the pain he had suffered and hoped that most of his life had been full of joy. I had been home about thirty minutes or so when Bayley's breathing slowed, sputtered, and then stopped. Dave and I sat with him for a bit longer as we imagined him leaving this world to find Leo and Spirit, whom he had loved and who had gone before him.

The other dogs—Sierra, Ichabod, Neeka, and Casper—all died within a year after Bayley's death. All our dogs, except Spirit, lived long, busy, happy lives, first with Gary and me, then with just me, and then with Dave and me. These wonderful dogs had all known Gary and had been an important link to him.

Gracie was the only dog that was left from our skijoring days, as she was several years younger than the others. By this time, Dave and I had separated our marriage, but not our friendship, and I often visited with him and Gracie. We had gone from a family with six dogs back to a family of one dog. Gracie had never been without other dogs in her life, and she howled the most heart-wrenching howl I had ever heard, over and over, day after day, following Casper's death. We would bring her in to be with us, and she would pace and ask to go back out. She seemed to be searching for the other dogs. She had been content when Casper had been the only dog with her, but she could not find contentment alone. We knew Gracie needed to have another dog.

Gracie

Dave and I traveled together to Glen Highland Farm, a couple of hours from our home, to see if Jesse, a Border Collie mix who had had several failed adoptions, might be right for our family. We let Gracie and Jesse meet each other in a fenced area at the farm, and they greeted each other and generally went their own ways. Jesse was focused on playing fetch with Dave, and Gracie was exploring her world. The owner of the rescue wondered if we might like to meet another of her dogs, another Border Collie mix. She was full of life and excitement. Dave had planned on adopting one dog during that visit, but we came home with two, Jesse and Darby. Gracie's mournful howling ceased.

Gracie became too frail to do any skijoring as she aged, but she still enjoyed running, rather stiff-legged, after her two new sisters, sometimes nipping them playfully as they danced by. She was nearly fourteen years old when she stopped eating.

With her death, a period of my life had ended. These amazing dogs—six of them, and then with Spirit's death, five, and then with the addition of Gracie, six again—had taught me so many things.

They taught me that you can experience joy and sadness at the same time. They taught me that you don't need to stop, even when things are turned upside down. They taught me that six dogs are really not too many.

Afterword

This was both a painful and joyful book to write. It was amazing to hear Gary's voice so clearly after all these years had passed since his death. Reading what he had written let me be with him again.

When Gary was near death, I told him I would finish his book. But, as I had wondered if he was going to write the book he said he was going to write, I wasn't really sure that I would finish the book I said I would finish. I would sometimes begin to read what he had written, and even write a bit, only to find myself unable to continue. I got on with life, filling it with work, music, photography, and adventure. It wasn't a bad thing to do.

Finally, though, something in me changed. I sat down to read what Gary had written, and suddenly the words came pouring out of my fingers, and I struggled to do anything *but* write. I found his meticulous notes and depended a great deal on them as I finished his book. And then, one by one, stories of my life with the dogs kept emerging, and I would smile (or cry, depending on the story) as I wrote.

I am in my seventies now, and Gary and the dogs have been gone from me for a long time. I feel, though, that this time with these very special dogs, interlinked with Gary's sickness and ultimate death, was an important era—a critical era—of my life. A time I must never forget. A period of time, unlike other times of my life, that somehow had a beginning, a middle, and an end.

It began with Leo and discovering skijoring. It ended when the last of our skijoring dogs died. There will never be anything like running silently behind my dogs through a beautiful, snowy wood. It is exhilarating. It is humbling. I long for it sometimes but have not returned to the sport since Gracie became too old to pull me. I am not sure why. It seems like that was a time for *then*. I am now in a time for *now*. But every now and then I look at the harnesses hanging in the garage...

I have a crazy, smart goldendoodle, who is everything I could want in a dog. But still I miss my skijoring dogs. Who knows? Maybe, just maybe, I'm ready for one more dog.

Betsy with Murphy and friend Peach

About the Author

Betsy Waterman is a New York State licensed psychologist and retired college professor who has never lived her adult life without a dog by her side. For nearly twenty years, she taught graduate level classes to school psychologists and school counselors-in-training and maintained a small private counseling practice in her home. While this book moves into an entirely different genre for her, she has co-edited and co-written other professional books and given scores of presentations at local, state, national, and international levels, including several popular presentations to schools and local clubs about sleddogging and skijoring. Even when fully involved in her professional career, her family and the dogs who shared her life were always at the center of all that she did. Since retiring, she has enjoyed improving her photography skills, learning to play the harp, and writing on social media about her crazy smart goldendoodle, Murphy, and their travels. And, did we mention that she really, really loves her chickens? And, of course, her sweet, gentle rescued cat, Mysty.

Find this and other great books at Simply Pets Books.

www.simplypetslifestyle.com

Lisa and the Pet Detectives

The Pet Detectives are an eleven-year-old English Labrador named Jaxxs, a fourteen-year-old yellow American Labrador named Blizzard, and a fifteen-year-old black English Labrador named Coopah! Their pet-mom is Lisa Smith Putnam, and together they make up Lisa and the Pet Detectives.

Lisa and the Pet Detectives are the owners and run Simply Pets Magazine by day, but they are always willing to lend a helping hand. They're always helping to solve problems and helping others find their way! Learning lessons while at play!

Mercury & Sirius

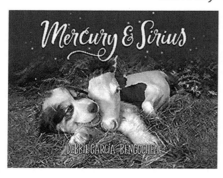

Sirius is a Maremma sheepdog, a livestock guardian breed from Italy. They are usually solid white dogs. But not Sirius; he was born with spots. When Sirius was two months old, Mercury was born on the farm. Mercury is a blue-eyed miniature horse. He has spots too, and an unusual color pattern with three white legs and one dark leg, one white ear and one dark ear.

Mercury and Sirius became instant friends. They may be different but only see the ways they are alike.

Simply Pets Books publishes books of interest to petparents—books that belong in the place where HAPPY lives!

We are building an eclectic inventory of genres, but all our titles are family friendly, uplifting, and involve animals in some way. If you love pets and enjoy reading HAPPY books, take a look at our other titles.

Simply Pets Books has two imprints: Simply Pets Books Traditional, a conventional publishing model, and Simply Pets Books Innovative, a collaborative publishing model. If you have written a book in which animals (or an animal) plays an important part, visit www.simplypetslifestyle.com and click on the Books tab.